THE S[ERVICE OF THE] SMAI[L PARAKLESIS] (INTERC[ESSORY PRAYER] TO THE MOST HOLY THEOTOKOS

ΑΚΟΛΟΥΘΙΑ ΤΟΥ ΜΙΚΡΟΥ ΠΑΡΑΚΛΗΤΙΚΟΥ ΚΑΝΟΝΟΣ ΕΙΣ ΤΗΝ ΥΠΕΡΑΓΙΑΝ ΘΕΟΤΟΚΟΝ

Translated and set to meter by
Demetri Kangelaris and Nicholas Kasemeotes

HOLY CROSS ORTHODOX PRESS
50 Goddard Avenue
Brookline, Massachusetts 02146

Revised, 1997
© Copyright 1984 HOLY CROSS ORTHODOX PRESS
Published by Holy Cross Orthodox Press
50 Goddard Avenue
Brookline, Massachusetts 02146

Library of Congress Cataloging in Publication Data

Orthodox Eastern Church
    The service of the small paraklesis, Intercessory prayer, to the
most Holy Theotokos=Akolouthia tou mikrou parakletikou kanonos
eis ten Hyperagian Theotokon.
    "A poem of the monk Theosterictus, but ascribed by others to
Theophanes."
    Translation of : Mikros paraklētikos kanōn.
    1. Orthodox Eastern Church. Mikros parakletikos kanōn—Texts.
2. Mary, Blessed Virgin, Saint—Prayer-books and devotions—Greek.
3. Mary, Blessed Virgin, Saint—Prayer-books and devotions—English.
4. Orthodox Eastern Church—Liturgy—Texts. 5. Greek Orthodox
Archdiocese of North and South America—Liturgy—Texts.
I. Theostēriktos, Monachos. II. Theophanēs, Hymnographos. III. Title.
IV. Title: Akolouthia tou mikrou paraklētikou kanonos eis tēn Hyper-
agian Theotokon.
BX375.M5307813 1984   264' .091907   84-12923
ISBN 0-917651-014 (pbk.)

Dedicated to the members of our families

A Helpful Key to the Transliteration

Except for a few irregularities, the vowels and consonants should be pronounced as they are in English. But please note the following:

ou   is always pronounced as in the word *through,* an *oo* sound.

i   is always pronounced as *ee,* as in the word *seat.*

h   is always (except when found in the *th* sound) pronounced as a *who* sound, as in the word *hard.*

a   is always pronounced as an *ah* sound, as in the word *hot.*

PUBLISHER'S NOTE

The service of the *Small Paraklesis,* conducted daily during the first fourteen days of August as well as on many other occasions, is one of the most popular services of the Orthodox Church. Until now, it was not always possible for all those who attended the services to participate in them fully because of the language difficulty. By providing, in addition to the original Greek text, an English *translation in meter* that fits the traditional *Byzantine melody,* and *a transliteration,* makes it possible for all Orthodox to participate fully.

Thus, it is with particular joy that Holy Cross Orthodox Press offers this edition of the *Paraklesis* to the Orthodox faithful, a labor of love on the part of Fathers Demetri Kangelaris and Nicholas Kasemeotes, recent graduates of Holy Cross Greek Orthodox School of Theology, now serving the Church in Los Angeles and St. Louis respectively.

Our special thanks then go to Fathers Demetri and Nicholas. May the Theotokos continue to bless them and their ministry and grant them every spiritual gift.

N. M. Vaporis
Director

TRANSLATORS' NOTE

It is with great joy and hope that we present this service book for use by our congregations. The service of the *Small Paraklesis* or "Intercessory Prayer" to the Most Holy Theotokos, the Mother of God, is chanted during the Lenten period of 1 to 14th August, preceding the Feast of the Koimesis or "Falling Asleep" of the Virgin Mary. The service is also chanted, as the prefix indicates, "in every tribulation and in sorrow of soul."

The purpose of this service book is to enable our congregations to participate more fully in the chanting of this service. The English phonetics have been provided along side of the Greek text to enable our non-Greek reading people to also chant the service. Second, an English translation has been provided which can be sung on the same melodic line as the Greek. Whether the service is sung in Greek or English, we encourage everyone to chant these very simple yet beautiful hymns and prayers.

We would like to acknowledge a previous translation, *The Service of Small Supplicatory Canon to the Most Holy Mother of God*, translated by the Holy Transfiguration Monastery, which was helpful in the formation of this translation. We would also like to thank members of the faculty of Hellenic College/Holy Cross Greek Orthodox School of Theology for their assistance: Fr. Alkiviadis Calivas, Professor Savas Savas, Dr. Penelope Tzougros, Mrs. Ioanna Clarke and Miss Georgia Stathopoulou.

We thank them and pray that through the prayers of the Theotokos, our Lord will bless them as well as all those who sing this service.

Demetri Kangelaris
Nicholas Kasemeotes

ΑΚΟΛΟΥΘΙΑ
ΤΟΥ ΜΙΚΡΟΥ
ΠΑΡΑΚΛΗΤΙΚΟΥ ΚΑΝΟΝΟΣ
ΕΙΣ ΤΗΝ ΥΠΕΡΑΓΙΑΝ ΘΕΟΤΟΚΟΝ
ΠΟΙΗΜΑ ΘΕΟΣΤΗΡΙΚΤΟΥ ΜΟΝΑΧΟΥ·
ΟΙ ΔΕ ΘΕΟΦΑΝΟΥΣ

(Ὁ Μικρὸς Παρακλητικὸς Κανὼν ψάλλεται ἐν πάσῃ περιστάσει καὶ θλίψει ψυχῆς καὶ κατὰ τὰς ἡμέρας τοῦ Δεκαπενταυγούστου.)

Ἱερεύς: Εὐλογητὸς ὁ Θεὸς ἡμῶν, πάντοτε· νῦν καὶ ἀεὶ καὶ εἰς τοὺς αἰῶνας τῶν αἰώνων.

Λαός: Ἀμήν.

Ψαλμὸς ρμβ΄ (142)

Κύριε, εἰσάκουσον τῆς προσευχῆς μου, ἐνώτισαι τὴν δέησίν μου ἐν τῇ ἀληθείᾳ σου, εἰσάκουσόν μου ἐν τῇ δικαιοσύνῃ σου. Καὶ μὴ εἰσέλθῃς εἰς

1

THE SERVICE OF THE SMALL PARAKLESIS TO THE MOST HOLY THEOTOKOS
BY THEOSTERIKTOS THE MONK, (OR THEOPHANES).

(The service of the Small Paraklesis is chanted in times of distress and sorrow of soul and during the first fourteen days of August.)

Priest: Blessed is our God always, now and forever and to the ages of ages.

People: Amen.

Psalm 142

O Lord, hear my prayer, give ear to my supplications in Your truth; hear me in Your righteousness.

1

κρίσιν μετὰ τοῦ δούλου σου, ὅτι οὐ δικαιωθήσεται ἐνώπιόν σου πᾶς ζῶν. Ὅτι κατεδίωξεν ὁ ἐχθρὸς τὴν ψυχήν μου· ἐταπείνωσεν εἰς γῆν τὴν ζωήν μου. Ἐκάθισέ με ἐν σκοτεινοῖς, ὡς νεκροὺς αἰῶνος· καὶ ἠκηδίασεν ἐπ᾽ ἐμὲ τὸ πνεῦμά μου, ἐν ἐμοὶ ἐταράχθη ἡ καρδία μου. Ἐμνήσθην ἡμερῶν ἀρχαίων, ἐμελέτησα ἐν πᾶσι τοῖς ἔργοις σου, ἐν ποιήμασι τῶν χειρῶν σου ἐμελέτων. Διεπέτασα πρὸς σὲ τὰς χεῖράς μου· ἡ ψυχή μου ὡς γῆ ἄνυδρός σοι. Ταχὺ εἰσάκουσόν μου, Κύριε· ἐξέλιπε τὸ πνεῦμά μου. Μὴ ἀποστρέψῃς τὸ πρόσωπόν σου ἀπ᾽ ἐμοῦ, καὶ ὁμοιωθήσομαι τοῖς καταβαίνουσιν εἰς λάκκον. Ἀκουστὸν ποίησόν μοι τὸ πρωῒ τὸ ἔλεός σου, ὅτι ἐπὶ σοὶ ἤλπισα. Γνώρισόν μοι, Κύριε, ὁδόν, ἐν ᾗ πορεύσομαι, ὅτι πρὸς σὲ ἦρα τὴν ψυχήν μου. Ἐξελοῦ με ἐκ τῶν ἐχθρῶν μου, Κύριε· πρὸς σὲ κατέφυγον· δίδαξόν με τοῦ ποιεῖν τὸ θέλημά σου, ὅτι σὺ εἶ ὁ Θεός μου. Τὸ Πνεῦμά σου τὸ ἀγαθὸν ὁδηγήσει με ἐν γῇ εὐθείᾳ· ἕνεκεν τοῦ ὀνόματός σου, Κύριε, ζήσεις με. Ἐν τῇ δικαιοσύνῃ σου ἐξάξεις ἐκ θλίψεως τὴν ψυχήν μου, καὶ ἐν τῷ ἐλέει σου ἐξολοθρεύσεις τοὺς ἐχθρούς μου. Καὶ ἀπολεῖς πάντας τοὺς θλίβοντας τὴν ψυχήν μου, ὅτι ἐγὼ δοῦλός σου εἰμί.

Ἦχος δ´

Θεὸς Κύριος καὶ ἐπέφανεν ἡμῖν· εὐλογημένος ὁ ἐρχόμενος ἐν ὀνόματι Κυρίου.

Στιχ. α´ Ἐξομολογεῖσθε τῷ Κυρίῳ καὶ ἐπικαλεῖσθε τὸ ὄνομα τὸ ἅγιον αὐτοῦ.

Θεὸς Κύριος καὶ ἐπέφανεν ἡμῖν· εὐλογημένος ὁ ἐρχόμενος ἐν ὀνόματι Κυρίου.

Do not enter into judgment, with Your servant, for in Your sight no one living is justified. For the enemy has persecuted my soul; he has crushed my life to the ground; he has made me dwell in darkness, like those who have long been dead, and my spirit is overwhelmed within me; my heart within me is distressed. I remembered the days of old; I meditated on all Your works: I pondered on the work of Your hands. I spread out my hands to You; my soul longs for You, like a thirsty land.

Hear me quickly, O Lord; my spirit fails. Do not turn Your face away from me, lest I be like those who go down into the pit. Cause me to hear Your mercy in the morning, for in You I have put my trust. Cause me to know, O Lord, the way in which I should walk, for I lift up my soul to You. Rescue me, Lord, from my enemies; to You have I fled for refuge. Teach me to do Your will, for You are my God. Your good Spirit shall lead me in the land of uprightness. For Your name's sake, O Lord, You shall quicken me. In Your righteousness You shall bring my soul out of trouble, and in Your mercy, You shall utterly destroy my enemies. And you shall destroy all those who afflict my soul; for I am Your servant.

Tone 4

God is the Lord; and has revealed Himself to us, blessed is he who comes in the name of the Lord.

Vs. 1. Give thanks to the Lord and call upon His holy name.

God is the Lord and has revealed Himself to us; blessed is he who comes in the name of the Lord.

Στιχ. β.΄ Πάντα τὰ ἔθνη ἐκύκλωσάν με, καὶ τῷ ὀνόματι Κυρίου ἠμυνάμην αὐτούς.

Θεὸς Κύριος καὶ ἐπέφανεν ἡμῖν· εὐλογημένος ὁ ἐρχόμενος ἐν ὀνόματι Κυρίου.

Στιχ. γ.΄ Παρὰ Κυρίου ἐγένετο αὕτη, καὶ ἔστι θαυμαστὴ ἐν ὀφθαλμοῖς ἡμῶν.

Θεὸς Κύριος καὶ ἐπέφανεν ἡμῖν· εὐλογημένος ὁ ἐρχόμενος ἐν ὀνόματι Κυρίου.

Ἦχος δ΄ Ὁ ὑψωθεὶς ἐν τῷ Σταυρῷ.

Τῇ Θεοτόκῳ ἐκτενῶς νῦν προσδράμωμεν, ἁμαρτωλοὶ καὶ ταπεινοὶ καὶ προσπέσωμεν ἐν μετανοίᾳ, κράζοντες ἐκ βάθους ψυχῆς· Δέσποινα, βοήθησον, ἐφ' ἡμῖν σπλαγχνισθεῖσα· σπεῦσον ἀπολλύμεθα, ὑπὸ πλήθους πταισμάτων· μὴ ἀποστρέψῃς σοὺς δούλους κενούς· σὲ γὰρ καὶ μόνην ἐλπίδα κεκτήμεθα.

Ti Theotoko ektenos nin prosdramomen, amartoli ke tapini, ke prospesomen en metania, krazondes ek vathous psihis; Despina, voithison, ef imin splahnisthisa; spefson, apolimetha, ipo plithous ptesmaton; mi apostrepsis sous doulous kenous; se gar ke monin elpida kektimetha.

Δόξα Πατρὶ καὶ Υἱῷ καὶ Ἁγίῳ Πνεύματι·

(Τὸ αὐτό, ἢ τὸ Ἀπολυτίκιον τοῦ Ἁγίου τοῦ Ναοῦ.)

Vs. 2. All the nations have surrounded me, but in the name of the Lord, I have overcome them.

God is the Lord and has revealed Himself to us; blessed is he who comes in the name of the Lord.

Vs. 3 This has been done by the Lord, and it is wonderful in our eyes.

God is the Lord and has revealed Himself to us; blessed is he who comes in the name of the Lord.

Tone 4

To the Theotokos, let us run now most fervently,
As sinners and lowly ones,
Let us fall down in repentance,
Crying from the depths of our soul:
Lady, come and help us,
Have compassion upon us;
Hasten now for we are lost
In the host of our errors;
Do not turn your servants away,
For you alone are a hope to us.

Glory to the Father and the Son and the Holy Spirit.

(Repeat the above or the Apolytikion of the Church.)

Καὶ νῦν καὶ ἀεὶ καὶ εἰς τοὺς αἰῶνας. Ἀμήν.

Οὐ σιωπήσωμέν ποτε, Θεοτόκε, τὰς δυναστεί-
ας σου λαλεῖν οἱ ἀνάξιοι· εἰμὴ γὰρ σὺ προΐστασο
πρεσβεύουσα, τὶς ἡμᾶς ἐρρύσατο ἐκ τοσούτων
κινδύνων; Τὶς δὲ διεφύλαξεν ἕως νῦν ἐλευθέρους;
Οὐκ ἀποστῶμεν, Δέσποινα, ἐκ σοῦ· σοὺς γὰρ δούλους σώζεις ἀεί, ἐκ παντοίων δεινῶν.

*Ou siopisomen pote, Theotoke, tas dinastias sou,
lalin i anaxii; imi gar si proistaso presvevousa, tis
imas erisato ek tosouton kindinon? Tis de diefilax-
sen eos nin eleftherous? Ouk apostomen, Despina,
ek sou; sous gar doulous sozis ai, ek pandion dinon.*

Ὁ Ἀναγνώστης (χῦμα)· Ψαλμὸς ν΄ (50).

Ἐλέησόν με ὁ Θεὸς κατὰ τὸ μέγα ἔλεός σου, καὶ
κατὰ τὸ πλῆθος τῶν οἰκτιρμῶν σου ἐξάλειψον τὸ
ἀνόμημά μου· Ἐπὶ πλεῖον πλῦνόν με ἀπὸ τῆς ἀ-
νομίας μου, καὶ ἀπὸ τῆς ἁμαρτίας μου καθάρι-
σόν με. Ὅτι τὴν ἀνομίαν μου ἐγὼ γινώσκω, καὶ
ἡ ἁμαρτία μου ἐνώπιόν μού ἐστι διὰ παντός. Σοὶ
μόνῳ ἥμαρτον, καὶ τὸ πονηρὸν ἐνώπιόν σου ἐποί-
ησα, ὅπως ἂν δικαιωθῇς ἐν τοῖς λόγοις σου, καὶ
νικήσῃς ἐν τῷ κρίνεσθαί σε. Ἰδοὺ γὰρ ἐν ἀνομί-
αις συνελήφθην, καὶ ἐν ἁμαρτίαις ἐκίσσησέ με ἡ
μήτηρ μου. Ἰδοὺ γὰρ ἀλήθειαν ἠγάπησας· τὰ ἄ-
δηλα καὶ τὰ κρύφια τῆς σοφίας σου ἐδήλωσάς μοι·
Ραντιεῖς με ὑσσώπῳ, καὶ καθαρισθήσομαι· πλυ-
νεῖς με, καὶ ὑπὲρ χιόνα λευκανθήσομαι. Ἀκουτι-

Now and forever and to the ages of ages. Amen.

O Theotokos, we shall never be silent.
Of your mighty acts, all we the unworthy;
Had you not stood to intercede for us
Who would have delivered us,
From the numerous perils?
Who would have preserved us all
Until now with our freedom?
O Lady, we shall not depart from you;
For you always save your servants,
From all tribulation.

Then we read: Psalm 50

Have mercy on me, O God, according to Your great mercy; and according to the multitude of Your compassion blot out my transgression. Wash me thoroughly from my iniquity, and cleanse me from my sin. For I acknowledge my iniquity, and my sin is ever before me. Against You, You only, have I sinned, and done this evil in Your sight, that You may be found just when You speak, and blameless when You judge. For behold, I was conceived in iniquity, and in sin my mother bore me.

For behold, You have loved truth: You have made known to me the secret things of Your wisdom. You shall sprinkle me with hyssop, and I shall be made clean: You shall wash me, and I shall

4

εἷς μοι ἀγαλλίασιν καὶ εὐφροσύνην· ἀγαλλιάσον-
ται ὀστέα τεταπεινωμένα. Ἀπόστρεψον τὸ πρόσωπόν σου ἀπὸ τῶν ἁμαρτιῶν μου, καὶ πάσας τὰς
ἀνομίας μου ἐξάλειψον. Καρδίαν καθαρὰν κτίσον
ἐν ἐμοὶ ὁ Θεός, καὶ Πνεῦμα εὐθὲς ἐγκαίνισον ἐν
τοῖς ἐγκάτοις μου. Μὴ ἀπορρίψῃς με ἀπὸ τοῦ προσώπου σου, καὶ τὸ Πνεῦμά σου τὸ Ἅγιον μὴ ἀν-
τανέλῃς ἀπ᾽ ἐμοῦ· Ἀπόδος μοι τὴν ἀγαλλίασιν
τοῦ σωτηρίου σου καὶ Πνεύματι ἡγεμονικῷ στή-
ριξόν με. Διδάξω ἀνόμους τὰς ὁδούς σου, καὶ ἀ-
σεβεῖς ἐπὶ σὲ ἐπιστρέψουσι. Ῥῦσαί με ἐξ αἱμάτων
ὁ Θεός, ὁ Θεὸς τῆς σωτηρίας μου· ἀγαλλιάσεται
ἡ γλῶσσά μου τὴν δικαιοσύνην σου. Κύριε, τὰ
χείλη μου ἀνοίξεις, καὶ τὸ στόμα μου ἀναγγελεῖ
τὴν αἴνεσίν σου. Ὅτι εἰ ἠθέλησας θυσίαν, ἔδωκα
ἄν· ὁλοκαυτώματα οὐκ εὐδοκήσεις. Θυσία τῷ
Θεῷ πνεῦμα συντετριμμένον· καρδίαν συντετριμ-
μένην καὶ τεταπεινωμένην ὁ Θεὸς οὐκ ἐξουδενώ-
σει. Ἀγάθυνον, Κύριε, ἐν τῇ εὐδοκίᾳ σου τὴν Σιών, καὶ οἰκοδομηθήτω τὰ τείχη Ἱερουσαλήμ. Τότε
εὐδοκήσεις θυσίαν δικαιοσύνης, ἀναφορὰν καὶ ὁ-
λοκαυτώματα. Τότε ἀνοίσουσιν ἐπὶ τὸ θυσιαστή-
ριόν σου μόσχους.

Ὠδὴ α΄. Ὁ Εἱρμός. Ἦχος πλ. δ΄.

Ὑγρὰν διοδεύσας ὡσεὶ ξηράν, καὶ τὴν αἰγυ-
πτίαν μοχθηρίαν διαφυγών, ὁ Ἰσραηλίτης ἀνε-
βόα· τῷ Λυτρωτῇ καὶ Θεῷ ἡμῶν ᾄσωμεν.

*Igran diodefsas osi xsiran, ke tin egiptian, moh-
thirian diafigon, o Israilitis anevoa; To Litroti ke
Theo imon asomen.*

5

be whiter than snow. Make me to hear joy and gladness, that bones which You have broken may rejoice. Turn Your face away from my sins, and blot out all my iniquities. Create in me a clean heart, O God, and renew a steadfast spirit within me. Do not cast me away from Your presence, and do not take Your Holy Spirit from me. Restore to me the joy of Your salvation: And establish me with Your governing Spirit.

I shall teach transgressors Your ways, and the ungodly shall turn back to You. Deliver me from bloodguiltiness, O God, the God of my salvation, my tongue shall rejoice in Your righteousness. O Lord, open my lips, and my mouth shall show forth Your praise. For if You had desired sacrifice, I would give it: You do not delight in burnt offering. A sacrifice to God is a broken spirit, God will not despise a broken and humbled heart.

Do good in Your good pleasure to Sion; and let the walls of Jerusalem be built. Then You shall be pleased with a sacrifice of righteousness, with oblation and whole burnt offerings. Then they shall offer bulls on Your altar.

Ode 1. The Heirmos. Plagal of the 4th Tone

Crossing the waters as on dry land,
In that way escaping
From the evils of Egypt's land,
The Israelites cried out exclaiming:
To our Redeemer and God, now let us sing.

Ὑπεραγία Θεοτόκε σῶσον ἡμᾶς.

Πολλοῖς συνεχόμενος πειρασμοῖς, πρὸς σὲ καταφεύγω, σωτηρίαν ἐπιζητῶν· Ὦ Μῆτερ τοῦ Λόγου, καὶ παρθένε, τῶν δυσχερῶν καὶ δεινῶν με
διάσωσον.

Polis sinehomenos pirazmis, pros se katafevgo,
sotirian epiziton; O Miter tou Logou, ke parthene,
ton disheron ke dinon me diasoson.

Ὑπεραγία Θεοτόκε σῶσον ἡμᾶς.

Παθῶν με ταράττουσι προσβολαί, πολλῆς ἀθυμίας, ἐμπιπλῶσαί μου τὴν ψυχήν· εἰρήνευσον, Κόρη τῇ γαλήνῃ, τῇ τοῦ Υἱοῦ καὶ Θεοῦ σου,
πανάμωμε.

Pathon me taratousi prosvole, polis athimias,
empiplose mou tin psihin; irinefson kori, ti galini,
ti tou Iou ke Theou sou, Panamome.

Δόξα Πατρὶ καὶ Υἱῷ καὶ Ἁγίῳ Πνεύματι.

Σωτῆρα τεκοῦσά σε καὶ Θεόν, δυσωπῶ, παρθένε, λυτρωθῆναί με τῶν δεινῶν· σοὶ γὰρ νῦν προσ-
φεύγων ἀνατείνω, καὶ τὴν ψυχὴν καὶ τὴν διάνοιαν.

Sotira tekousa se ke Theon, disopo, Parthene,
litrothine me ton dinon; si gar nin prosfevgon ana-
tino, ke tin psihin ke tin dianian.

Most Holy Theotokos save us.

With many temptations surrounding me,
Searching for salvation,
I have hastened unto you;
O Mother of the Word, and ever-Virgin,
From all distresses and dangers deliver me.

Most Holy Theotokos save us.

Assaults of the passions have shaken me,
My soul to its limits
Has been filled with much despair;
Bring peace, O Maiden, in the calmness,
Of your own Son and your God, all-blameless One.

Glory to the Father and the Son and the Holy Spirit.

To God and the Savior you've given birth;
I ask you, O Virgin,
From the dangers deliver me;
For now I run to you for refuge,
With both my soul and my reasoning.

Καὶ νῦν καὶ ἀεὶ καὶ εἰς τοὺς αἰῶνας τῶν αἰώνων.

Νοσοῦντα τὸ σῶμα καὶ τὴν ψυχήν, ἐπισκοπῆς θείας, καὶ προνοίας τῆς παρὰ σοῦ, ἀξίωσον μόνη Θεομῆτορ, ὡς ἀγαθὴ ἀγαθοῦ τε λοχεύτρια.

Nosounda to soma ke tin psihin, episkopis thias, ke pronias tis para sou, axsioson moni Theomitor, os agathi agathou te loheftria.

'Ωδὴ γ΄ 'Ο Εἱρμός.

Οὐρανίας ἀψῖδος ὀροφουργὲ Κύριε, καὶ τῆς 'Εκκλησίας δομῆτορ, σύ με στερέωσον, ἐν τῇ ἀγάπῃ τῇ σῇ, τῶν ἐφετῶν ἡ ἀκρότης, τῶν πιστῶν τὸ στήριγμα, μόνε φιλάνθρωπε.

Ouranias apsidòs orofourge Kirie, ke tis Eklisias domitor, si me stereoson, en ti agapi ti si, ton efeton i akrotis, ton piston to stirigma, mone filanthrope.

'Υπεραγία Θεοτόκε σῶσον ἡμᾶς.

Προστασίαν καὶ σκέπην, ζωῆς ἐμῆς τίθημι, Σὲ θεογεννῆτορ Παρθένε· σύ με κυβέρνησον, πρὸς τὸν λιμένα σου, τῶν ἀγαθῶν ἡ αἰτία, τῶν πιστῶν τὸ στήριγμα, μόνη πανύμνητε.

Prostasian ke skepin, zois emis tithimi, se Theogenitor Parthene; si me kivernison, pros ton limena sou, ton agathon i etia, ton piston to stirigma, moni panimnite.

Now and forever, and to the ages of ages. Amen.

Diseased is the body and the soul;
Deem me truly worthy
Of divine guidance and your care;
For you alone are God's Mother,
As the good and the birthgiver of the Good.

Ode 3. The Heirmos.

The apse of the heavens,
Are you O Lord, Fashioner,
And the Holy Church's great Founder,
Likewise establish me,
In constant love for You
For You're the height of our longing;
Support of the faithful,
The only Friend of all.

Most Holy Theotokos save us.

A protection and shelter,
I have with you in my life,
You, the Theotokos and the Virgin,
Pilot me towards your port;
For you are the cause,
The cause of that which is good,
Support of the faithful,
The only all-praised One.

Ὑπεραγία Θεοτόκε σῶσον ἡμᾶς.

Ἱκετεύω Παρθένε, τὸν ψυχικὸν τάραχον, καὶ τῆς ἀθυμίας τὴν ζάλην διασκεδάσαι μου· σὺ γάρ, θεόνυμφε, τον ἀρχηγὸν τῆς γαλήνης, τὸν Χριστὸν ἐκύησας, μόνη πανάχραντε.

Iketevo Parthene, ton psihikon tarahon, ke tis athimias tin zalin diaskedase mou; si gar, theonimfe, ton arhigon tis galinis, ton Hriston ekiisas moni panahrande.

Δόξα Πατρὶ καὶ Υἱῷ καὶ Ἁγίῳ Πνεύματι.

Εὐεργέτην τεκοῦσα, τὸν τῶν καλῶν αἴτιον, τῆς εὐεργεσίας τὸν πλοῦτον, πᾶσιν ἀνάβλυσον· πάντα γὰρ δύνασαι, ὡς δυνατὸν ἐν ἰσχύϊ, τὸν Χριστὸν κυήσασα, θεομακάριστε.

Evergetin tekousa, ton to kalon etion, tis evergesias ton plouton, pasin anavlison; panda gar dinase, os dinaton en ishii, ton Hriston kiisasa, theomakariste.

Καὶ νῦν καὶ ἀεὶ καὶ εἰς τοὺς αἰῶνας τῶν αἰώνων.

Χαλεπαῖς ἀρρωστίαις, καὶ νοσεροῖς πάθεσιν, ἐξεταζομένῳ Παρθένε, σύ μοι βοήθησον· τῶν ἰαμάτων γὰρ ἀνελλιπῆ σε γινώσκω, θησαυρὸν πανάμωμε, τὸν ἀδαπάνητον.

Halepes arosties, ke noseris pathesin, exsetazomeno Parthene, si mi voithison; ton iamaton gar, anelipi se ginosko, thisavron panamome, ton adapaniton.

Most Holy Theotokos save us.

I entreat you, O Virgin,
Disperse the storm of my grief,
and the soul's most inward confusion,
Scatter it far from me;
You are the Bride of God,
For you have brought forth the Christ,
the Prince of Peace;
Only, all-blameless One.

Glory to the Father and the Son and the Holy Spirit.

Having brought forth unto us
the cause and giver of good,
From your great abundance of kindness,
Pour forth upon us all;
For all is possible,
For you who carried the Christ,
Who is mighty in power;
You, who are blessed of God.

Now and forever and to the ages of ages. Amen

With most serious ailments,
And with the passions so dark,
I am being tested, O Virgin,
Come and bring help to me;
For I have known of you,
That you are without fail
the endless treasure of cures,
Only all-blameless One.

Διάσωσον, ἀπὸ κινδύνων τοὺς δούλους σου Θεοτόκε, ὅτι πάντες μετὰ Θεὸν εἰς σὲ καταφεύγομεν, ὡς ἄρρηκτον τεῖχος καὶ προστασίαν.

Diasoson, apo kindinon tous doulous sou Theotoke, oti pandes meta Theon is se katafevgomen, os arikton tihos ke prostasian.

Ἐπίβλεψον, ἐν εὐμενείᾳ πανύμνητε Θεοτόκε, ἐπὶ τὴν ἐμὴν χαλεπὴν τοῦ σώματος κάκωσιν, καὶ ἴασαι τῆς ψυχῆς μου τὸ ἄλγος.

Epivlepson, en evmenia panimnite Theotoke, epi tin emin halepin tou somatos kakosin, ke iase tis psihis mou to algos.

(Καὶ μνημονεύει ὁ Ἱερεὺς ἐκείνων, δι' οὓς ἡ παράκλησις τελεῖται.)

Ἱερεύς: Ἐλέησον ἡμᾶς ὁ Θεός, κατὰ τὸ μέγα ἔλεός σου, δεόμεθά σου, ἐπάκουσον καὶ ἐλέησον.

Λαός: Κύριε, ἐλέησον (3).

Ἱερεύς: Ἔτι δεόμεθα, ὑπὲρ τοῦ Ἀρχιεπισκόπου ἡμῶν *(ὄνομα)* καὶ τοῦ Ἐπισκόπου ἡμῶν *(ὄνομα)* καὶ πάσης τῆς ἐν Χριστῷ ἡμῶν ἀδελφότητος.

Λαός: Κύριε, ἐλέησον *(3).*

Deliver us,
All of your servants, from danger, O Theotokos;
After God, we all flee to you,
For shelter and covering,
As an unshakable wall and our protection.

Turn to me,
In your good favor, all praise-worthy Theotokos;
Look upon my grave illnesses,
Which painfully sting my flesh
and heal the cause of my soul's pain and suffering.

(The priest commemorates those for whom the Paraklesis is sung.)

Priest: Have mercy on us, O God, according to Your great love, we pray You, hearken, and have mercy.

People: Lord have mercy (*3*).

Priest: Again we pray for our Archbishop (*name*), our Bishop (*name*), and all the clergy and the laity in Christ.

People: Lord have mercy (*3*).

Ἱερεύς: Ἔτι δεόμεθα, ὑπὲρ ἐλέους, ζωῆς, εἰρήνης, ὑγείας, σωτηρίας, ἐπισκέψεως, συγχωρήσεως καὶ ἀφέσεως τῶν ἁμαρτιῶν, τῶν δούλων τοῦ Θεοῦ πάντων τῶν εὐσεβῶν καὶ ὀρθοδόξων χριστιανῶν, τῶν κατοικούντων καὶ παρεπιδημούντων ἐν τῇ πόλει (ἢ *νήσῳ*) ταύτῃ, τῶν ἐνοριτῶν, ἐπιτρόπων, συνδρομητῶν καὶ ἀφιερωτῶν τοῦ ἁγίου Ναοῦ τούτου.

Λαός: Κύριε, ἐλέησον (3).

Ἱερεύς: Ἔτι δεόμεθα καὶ ὑπὲρ τῶν δούλων τοῦ Θεοῦ (*καὶ μνημονεύει ὀνομαστὶ τῶν δι' οὓς ἡ παράκλησις τελεῖται*).

Λαός: Κύριε, ἐλέησον (3).

Ἱερεύς: Ὅτι ἐλεήμων καὶ φιλάνθρωπος Θεὸς ὑπάρχεις καὶ Σοὶ τὴν δόξαν ἀναπέμπομεν τῷ Πατρί, καὶ τῷ Υἱῷ καὶ τῷ Ἁγίῳ Πνεύματι, νῦν καὶ ἀεὶ καὶ εἰς τοὺς αἰῶνας τῶν αἰώνων.

Λαός: Ἀμήν.

(Μετὰ τὴν δέησιν τὸ ἐπόμενον Κάθισμα.)
Ἦχος β´ Τὰ ἄνω ζητῶν.

Πρεσβεία θερμή, καὶ τεῖχος ἀπροσμάχητον, ἐλέους πηγή, τοῦ κόσμου καταφύγιον, ἐκτενῶς βοῶμέν σοι· Θεοτόκε Δέσποινα, πρόφθασον, καὶ ἐκ κινδύνων λύτρωσαι ἡμᾶς, ἡ μόνη ταχέως προστατεύουσα.

Presvia thermi, ke tihos aprosmahiton, eleous pigi, tou kosmou katafigion, ektenos voomen si; Theotoke Despina, profthason, ke ek kindinon litrose imas, i moni taheos prostatevousa.

Priest: Again we pray for mercy, life, peace, health, salvation, visitation, forgiveness and remission of the sins of the servants of God, all pious and Orthodox Christians, those who reside and visit in this city, the members, council members, contributors, and benefactors of this holy church.

People: Lord have mercy (*3*).

Priest: Again we pray for the servants of God. . . (*At this time the Priest commemorates those for whom the Paraklesis is sung.*)

People: Lord have mercy (*3*).

For You are a merciful and loving God, and to You we give glory, to the Father and the Son and the Holy Spirit, now and forever and to the ages of ages.

People: Amen.

(*After the petitions, we chant the following Kathisma:*)

Tone 2.

A fervent prayer, and wall most unshakable
A merciful spring
And shelter of all mankind;
Fervently, we cry to you:
Theotokos, our Lady,
Come to us
And from all dangers now deliver us
The only protection who speeds to us.

'Ωδὴ δ΄ Ὁ Εἱρμός.

Εἰσακήκοα Κύριε, τῆς οἰκονομίας σου τὸ μυ-
στήριον· κατενόησα τὰ ἔργα σου, καὶ ἐδόξασά
σου τὴν θεότητα.

Isakikoa Kirie, tis ikonomias sou to mistirion;
katenoisa ta erga sou, ke edoxsasa sou tin theotita.

Ὑπεραγία Θεοτόκε σῶσον ἡμᾶς.

Τῶν παθῶν μου τὸν τάραχον, ἡ τὸν κυβερνή-
την τεκοῦσα Κύριον, καὶ τὸν κλύδωνα κατεύνα-
σον, τῶν ἐμῶν πταισμάτων θεονύμφευτε.

Ton pathon mou ton tarahon, i ton kivernitin
tekousa kirion, ke ton klidona katevnason, ton emon
ptesmaton theonumfefte.

Ὑπεραγία Θεοτόκε σῶσον ἡμᾶς.

Εὐσπλαγχνίας τὴν ἄβυσσον, ἐπικαλουμένῳ
τῆς σῆς παράσχου μοι, ἡ τὸν εὔσπλαγχνον κυήσασα, καὶ Σωτῆρα πάντων τῶν ὑμνούντων σε.

Efsplahnias tin avison, epikaloumeno tis sis pa-
rashou mi, i ton efsplahnon kiisasa, ke sotira pan-
don ton imnoundon se.

11

Ode 4. The Heirmos.

O Lord, I have heard of
the wondrous mystery
of Your salvation;
I have contemplated all Your works
And I have glorified Your great divinity.

Most Holy Theotokos, save us.

Still the darkest of passions,
Calm the sea of errors
In your great peacefulness;
It was you who bore the guiding Lord,
And you who are the blessed bride of God.

Most Holy Theotokos save us.

Your depth of compassion
Grant unto me
As one beseeching you;
You have carried the Compassionate
The Savior of those praising you.

Δόξα Πατρὶ καὶ Υἱῷ καὶ Ἁγίῳ Πνεύματι.

Ἀπολαύοντες Πάναγνε, τῶν σῶν δωρημάτων εὐχαριστήριον, ἀναμέλπομεν ἐφύμνιον, οἱ γινώσκοντές σε θεομήτορα.

Apolavondes panagne, ton son dorimaton efharistirion, anamelpomen efimnion, i ginoskondes se theomitora.

Καὶ νῦν καὶ ἀεὶ καὶ εἰς τοὺς αἰῶνας τῶν αἰώνων. Ἀμήν.

Οἱ ἐλπίδα καὶ στήριγμα, καὶ τῆς σωτηρίας τεῖχος ἀκράδαντον, κεκτημένοι σε πανύμνητε, δυσχερείας πάσης ἐκλυτρούμεθα.

I elpida ke stirigma, ke tis sotirias tihos akradandon, kektimeni se panimnite, diskerias pasis eklitroumetha.

Ὠδὴ ε΄ Ὁ Εἱρμός.

Φώτισον ἡμᾶς, τοῖς προστάγμασί σου, Κύριε, καὶ τῷ βραχίονί σου τῷ ὑψηλῷ, τὴν σὴν εἰρήνην, παράσχου ἡμῖν φιλάνθρωπε.

Fotison imas, tis prostagmasi sou, Kirie, ke to vrahioni sou to ipsilo, tin sin irinin, paraskou imin filanthrope.

Glory to the Father and the Son and the Holy Spirit.

We are thankful for all the gifts
Which we have been given
by you the Spotless One;
And to you, we sing a hymn of praise,
Knowing you to be the Mother of God.

Now and forever and to the ages of ages. Amen.

As a hope and foundation,
And a wall unshaken
Of our salvation;
Having you, the all-lauded One,
From afflictions do you rescue us.

Ode 5. The Heirmos.

Lord, enlighten us,
With Your precepts that can guide our lives,
And with Your arm most powerful
Grant to us Your peace,
O You Who are the Friend of all.

Ὑπεραγία Θεοτόκε σῶσον ἡμᾶς.

Ἔμπλησον ἀγνή, εὐφροσύνης τὴν καρδίαν μου, τὴν σὴν ἀκήρατον διδοῦσα χαράν, τῆς εὐφροσύνης ἡ γεννήσασα τὸν αἴτιον.

Emblison agni, efrosinis tin kardian mou, tin sin akiraton didousa haran, tis efrosinis i genisasa ton etion.

Ὑπεραγία Θεοτόκε σῶσον ἡμᾶς.

Λύτρωσαι ἡμᾶς, ἐκ κινδύνων Θεοτόκε, ἁγνή, ἡ αἰωνίαν τεκοῦσα λύτρωσιν, καὶ τὴν εἰρήνην τὴν πάντα νοῦν ὑπερέχουσαν.

Litrose imas, ek kindinon Theotoke, agni, i eonian tekousa litrosin, ke tin irinin tin panda noun iperexousan.

Δόξα Πατρὶ καὶ Υἱῷ καὶ Ἁγίῳ Πνεύματι.

Λῦσον τὴν ἀχλύν, τῶν πταισμάτων μου, θεόνυμφε, τῷ φωτισμῷ τῆς σῆς λαμπρότητος, ἡ φῶς τεκοῦσα τὸ θεῖον καὶ προαιώνιον.

Lison tin ahlin ton ptesmaton mou, theonimfe, to fotismo tis sis lambrotitos, i fos tekousa to thion ke proeonion.

Most Holy Theotokos, save us.

Pure one, fill my heart
with a merriment, a happiness;
Bestow on me your spotless joy,
For you have given birth
to Him Who is the cause of joy.

Most Holy Theotokos, save us.

Deliver all of us
From the dangers, Theotokos, most pure,
For you bore the timeless deliverer,
And you bore the peace,
the peace which has surpassed all thought.

Glory to the Father and the Son and the Holy Spirit.

Dissipate the cloud
Of my sinfulness, O bride of God,
With the brightness of your eminence;
For you brought forth the Light,
The Divine, which was before all time.

Καὶ νῦν καὶ ἀεὶ καὶ εἰς τοὺς αἰῶνας τῶν αἰώνων. Ἀμήν.

Ἴασαι ἁγνή, τῶν παθῶν μου τὴν ἀσθένειαν, ἐπισκοπῆς σου ἀξιώσασα, καὶ τὴν ὑγείαν τῇ πρεσβείᾳ σου παράσχου μοι.

Iase agni, ton pathon mou tin asthenian, episkopis sou axsiosasa, ke tin igian ti presvia sou parashou mi.

Ὠδὴ ς΄ Ὁ Εἱρμός.

Τὴν δέησιν ἐκχεῶ πρὸς Κύριον, καὶ αὐτῷ ἀπαγγελῶ μου τὰς θλίψεις· ὅτι κακῶν, ἡ ψυχή μου ἐπλήσθη, καὶ ἡ ζωή μου τῷ ᾅδῃ προσήγγισε καὶ δέομαι ὡς Ἰωνᾶς· Ἐκ φθορᾶς ὁ Θεός με ἀνάγαγε.

Tin deisin ekheo pros Kirion, ke afto apangelo mou tas thlipsis; oti kakon, i psihi mou eplisthi, ke i zoi mou to adi prosingise ke deome os Ionas; Ek fthoras o Theos me anagage.

Ὑπεραγία Θεοτόκε σῶσον ἡμᾶς.

Θανάτου καὶ τῆς φθορᾶς ὡς ἔσωσεν, ἑαυτὸν ἐκδεδωκὼς τῷ θανάτῳ, τὴν τῇ φθορᾷ, καὶ θανάτῳ μου φύσιν, κατασχεθεῖσαν Παρθένε, δυσώπησον, τὸν Κύριόν σου καὶ Υἱόν, τοῖς ἐχθρῶν κακουργίας με ῥύσασθαι.

Thanatou ke tis fthoras os esosen, eafton ekdedokos to thanato, tin ti fthora, ke thanato mou fisin, katestisan Parthene disopison, ton Kirion sou ke Ion, tis ehthron kakourgias me risasthe.

Now and for ever and to the ages of ages. Amen.

Heal me from the ills
O Most Pure One which the passions bring,
Make me worthy of your guiding care,
And unto me grant health,
Through your intercessions and your prayers.

Ode 6. The Heirmos.

My petition, I pour out to the Lord,
And to Him I will confess all my sorrows;
For many woes
Fill my soul to its limits,
And unto Hades my whole life has now approached,
Like Jonah, I pray to You,
From corruption, O God, now raise me

Most Holy Theotokos, save us.

From death and corruption He has saved
My nature, held by death and corruption;
For unto death
He Himself has surrendered;
For which reason, O Virgin, please intercede
With Him who is your Lord and Son,
From the enemies' evils deliver me.

Ὑπεραγία Θεοτόκε σῶσον ἡμᾶς.

Προστάτιν σε τῆς ζωῆς ἐπίσταμαι, καὶ φρου-
ρὰν ἀσφαλεστάτην Παρθένε τῶν πειρασμῶν, δι-
αλύουσαν ὄχλον, καὶ ἐπηρείας δαιμόνων ἐλαύνου-
σαν· καὶ δέομαι διαπαντός, ἐκ φθορᾶς τῶν παθῶν
μου ρυσθῆναί με.

Prostatin se tis zois epistame, ke frouran asfa-
lestatin Parthene, ton pirasmon, dialiousan ohlon,
ke epirias demonon elavnousan; ke deome diapan-
dos, ek fthoras ton pathon mou risthine me.

Δόξα Πατρὶ καὶ Υἱῷ καὶ Ἁγίῳ Πνεύματι.

Ὡς τεῖχος καταφυγῆς κεκτήμεθα, καὶ ψυχῶν
σε παντελῆ σωτηρίαν, καὶ πλατυσμόν, ἐν ταῖς θλί-
ψεσι, Κόρη, καὶ τῷ φωτί σου ἀεί, ἀγαλλόμεθα. Ὦ
Δέσποινα καὶ νῦν ἡμᾶς, τῶν παθῶν καὶ κινδύνων
διάσωσον.

Os tihos katafigis kektimetha, ke psihon se
pandeli sotirian, ke platismon, em tes thlipsesi, Kori,
ke to foti sou ai, agalometha. O Despina ke nin imas,
ton pathon ke kindinon diasoson.

Καὶ νῦν καὶ ἀεὶ καὶ εἰς τοὺς αἰῶνας τῶν αἰώνων.
Ἀμήν.

Ἐν κλίνῃ νῦν ἀσθενῶν κατάκειμαι, καὶ οὐκ
ἔστιν ἴασις τῇ σαρκί μου· ἀλλ᾽ ἡ Θεὸν καὶ σωτῆρα
τοῦ κόσμου, καὶ τὸν λυτῆρα τῶν νόσων κυήσασα,
σοῦ δέομαι τῆς ἀγαθῆς· Ἐκ φθορᾶς τῶν
νοσημάτων ἀνάστησον.

En klini nin asthenon katakime, ke ouk estin iasis
ti sarki mou: al i Theon, ke sotira tou kosmou, ke
ton litira ton noson kiisasa, sou deome tis agathis;
Ek fthoras nosimaton anastison.

Most Holy Theotokos, save us.

I know you as the protection of my life,
A steadfast shelter and refuge, O Virgin;
Disperse the host
Of my many temptations,
And force away the demonic attacks from me;
I pray to you unceasingly,
From corruption of passions deliver me.

Glory to the Father and the Son and the Holy Spirit.

We have you as a wall of refuge,
And our soul's most perfect salvation;
You are an aid,
In affliction, O Maiden,
And in your light we rejoice to eternity;
O Lady, also now,
From the passions and dangers deliver us.

Now and forever and to the ages of ages. Amen.

I lie now on a bed of infirmities,
And there is no healing at all for my body
Except for you,
Who has brought forth our Savior,
God, the healer of all our infirmities;
Of your goodness, I pray to you,
From corruption of sicknesses raise me.

Διάσωσον, ἀπὸ κινδύνων τοὺς δούλους σου Θεοτόκε, ὅτι πάντες μετὰ Θεὸν εἰς σὲ καταφεύγομεν, ὡς ἄρρηκτον τεῖχος καὶ προστασίαν.

Diasoson, apo kindinon tous doulous sou, Theotoke, oti pandes meta Theon is se katafevgomen, os arikton tihos ke prostasian.

Ἄχραντε, ἡ διὰ λόγου τὸν Λόγον ἀνερμηνεύτως, ἐπ᾽ ἐσχάτων τῶν ἡμερῶν τεκοῦσα, δυσώπησον, ὡς ἔχουσα μητρικὴν παρρησίαν.

Ahrande, i dia logou ton Logon anermineftos, ep eshaton ton imeron tekousa, disopison, os ehousa mitrikin parisian.

Ὁ Ἱερεὺς μνημονεύει ὡς δεδήλωται.
Κοντάκιον. Ἦχος β´

Προστασία τῶν Χριστιανῶν ἀκαταίσχυντε, μεσιτεία πρὸς τὸν ποιητὴν ἀμετάθετε, μὴ παρίδῃς ἁμαρτωλῶν δεήσεων φωνάς· ἀλλὰ πρόφθασον, ὡς ἀγαθή, εἰς τὴν βοήθειαν ἡμῶν, τῶν πιστῶς κραυγαζόντων σοι· Τάχυνον εἰς πρεσβείαν καὶ σπεῦσον εἰς ἱκεσίαν, ἡ προστατεύουσα ἀεί, Θεοτόκε τῶν τιμώντων σε.

Prostasia ton Xristianon akateshinde, mesitia pros ton piitin ametathete, mi paridis amartolon deiseon fonas: ala profthason, os agathi, is tin boithian imon, ton pistos kravgazondon si: Tahinon is presvian ke spefson is ikesian, i prostatevousa ai, Theotoke ton timondon se.

Deliver us,
All of your servants, from dangers, O Theotokos;
After God, we all flee to you,
For shelter and covering,
As an unshakable wall and our protection.

Spotless one,
Who by a word, did bring to us the Word eternal,
In the last days ineffably;
Do you now plead with him
As the one with the motherly favor.

The priest commemorates as before.
Kondakion. Tone 2.

A protection of Christians unshamable,
Intercessor to our Holy Maker, unwavering,
Please reject not
The prayerful cries of those who are in sin.
Instead, come to us, for you are good;
Your loving help bring unto us,
Who are crying in faith to you:
Hasten to intercede
And speed now to supplicate,
As a protection for all time,
Theotokos, for those who honor you.

(Εἶτα τὸ πρῶτον Ἀντίφωνον τῶν Ἀναβαθμῶν τοῦ δ.´ Ἦχου.)

Ἐκ νεότητός μου πολλὰ πολεμεῖ με πάθη· ἀλλ᾽ αὐτὸς ἀντιλαβοῦ, καὶ σῶσον, Σωτήρ μου (2).

Ek neotitos mou, pola polemi me pathi al aftos andilavou, ke soson, Sotir mou.

Οἱ μισοῦντες Σιών, αἰσχύνθητε ἀπὸ τοῦ Κυρίου· ὡς χόρτος γάρ, πυρὶ ἔσεσθε ἀπεξηραμμένοι (2).

I misoundes Sion, eshinthite apo tou Kiriou; os hortos gar, piri esesthe apexirameni.

Δόξα Πατρὶ καὶ Υἱῷ καὶ Ἁγίῳ Πνεύματι.

Ἁγίῳ Πνεύματι, πᾶσα ψυχὴ ζωοῦται, καὶ καθάρσει ὑψοῦται, λαμπρύνεται, τῇ Τριαδικῇ μονάδι ἱεροκρυφίως.

Agio Pnevmati, pasa psihi zooute, ke katharsi, ipsoute, lambrinete, ti Triadiki monadi, ierokrifios.

Καὶ νῦν καὶ ἀεὶ καὶ εἰς τοὺς αἰῶνας τῶν αἰώνων. Ἀμήν.

Ἁγίῳ Πνεύματι ἀναβλύζει τὰ τῆς χάριτος, ῥεῖθρα ἀδρεύοντα ἅπασαν τὴν κτίσιν, πρὸς ζωογονίαν.

Agio Pnevmati, anavlizi, ta tis haritos, rithra, adrevonda apasan tin ktisin, pros zoogonian.

Μνησθήσομαι τοῦ ὀνόματός σου ἐν πάσῃ γενεᾷ καὶ γενεᾷ.

Mnisthisome tou onomatos sou en pasi genea ke genea.

From the years of my youth,many passions combat me; but You, Who are my Savior, assist me and save me. (2)

You haters of Zion shall be put to shame by the Lord Almighty, for as grass in the fire, you shall all be withered. (2)

Glory to the Father and the Son and the Holy Spirit.

By the Holy Spirit, every soul is made living, is exalted, and made shining through purification, by the Threefold Oneness, in a hidden manner.

Now and for ever and to the ages of ages. Amen.

By the Holy Spirit, the streams of grace are flowing, watering, all of the creation, granting life upon

I shall remember your Holy Name from generation to generation.

Στιχ. Ἄκουσον, Θύγατερ, καὶ ἴδε, καὶ κλῖνον τὸ οὖς σου, καὶ ἐπιλάθου τοῦ λαοῦ σου, καὶ τοῦ οἴκου τοῦ πατρός σου καὶ ἐπιθυμήσει ὁ Βασιλεὺς τοῦ κάλλους σου.

Μνησθήσομαι τοῦ ὀνόματός σου ἐν πάσῃ γενεᾷ καὶ γενεᾷ.

Ἱερεύς: Καὶ ὑπὲρ τοῦ καταξιωθῆναι ἡμᾶς τῆς ἀκροάσεως τοῦ ἁγίου Εὐαγγελίου, Κύριόν τὸν Θεὸν ἡμῶν ἱκετεύσωμεν.

Λαός: Κύριε, ἐλέησον (3).

Ἱερεύς: Σοφία· ὀρθοί, ἀκούσωμεν τοῦ ἁγίου Εὐαγγελίου. Εἰρήνη πᾶσι.

Λαός: Καὶ τῷ Πνεύματί σου.

Ἱερεύς: Ἐκ τοῦ κατὰ Λουκᾶν ἁγίου Εὐαγγελίου, τὸ Ἀνάγνωσμα. Πρόσχωμεν.

Λαός: Δόξα σοι, Κύριε, δόξα σοι.

Ἱερεύς: Ἐν ταῖς ἡμέραις ἐκείναις, ἀναστᾶσα Μαριάμ, ἐπορεύθη εἰς τὴν ὀρεινὴν μετὰ σπουδῆς, εἰς πόλιν Ἰούδα· καὶ εἰσῆλθεν εἰς τὸν οἶκον Ζαχαρίου, καὶ ἠσπάσατο τὴν Ἐλισάβετ. Καὶ ἐγένετο, ὡς ἤκουσεν ἡ Ἐλισάβετ τὸν ἀσπασμὸν τῆς Μαρίας, ἐσκίρτησε τὸ βρέφος ἐν τῇ κοιλίᾳ αὐτῆς· καὶ ἐπλήσθη Πνεύματος Ἁγίου ἡ Ἐλισάβετ, καὶ ἀνεφώνησε φωνῇ μεγάλῃ, καὶ εἶπεν· Εὐλογημένη σὺ ἐν γυναιξὶ καὶ εὐλογημένος ὁ καρπὸς τῆς κοιλίας σου. Καὶ πόθεν μοι τοῦτο, ἵνα ἔλθῃ ἡ μήτηρ τοῦ Κυρίου μου πρός με; Ἰδοὺ γάρ, ὡς ἐγένετο ἡ φωνὴ τοῦ ἀσπασμοῦ σου εἰς τὰ ὦτά μου, ἐσκίρτησε τὸ βρέφος ἐν ἀγαλλιάσει ἐν τῇ κοιλίᾳ μου. Καὶ μακαρία ἡ πιστεύσασα, ὅτι ἔσται τελείωσις τοῖς

Verse: Listen, O Daughter, and see, and incline your ear, and forget your people and your father's house and the King will desire your beauty.

I remember Your Holy Name from generation to generation.

Priest: Let us pray to the Lord, our God, that we may be deemed worthy to hear the Holy Gospel,

People: Lord, have mercy (*3*).

Priest: Wisdom, Arise, Let us hear the Holy Gospel. Peace be with all.

People: And with your spirit.

Priest: The reading of the Holy Gospel according to Luke. Let us be attentive.

People: Glory to You, O Lord, glory to You.

Priest: In those days Mary arose and went in haste into the hill country, to a city of Judah, and she entered the house of Zachariah and greeted Elizabeth. And when Elizabeth heard the greeting of Mary, the babe leaped in her womb; and Elizabeth was filled with the Holy Spirit and she exclaimed with a loud cry, "Blessed are you among women, and blessed is the fruit of your womb! And why is this granted me, that the mother of my Lord should come to me? For behold, when the voice of your greeting came to my ears, the babe in my womb leaped for joy. And blessed is she who believed, for there would be a fulfillment of what was spoken to her from the Lord." And Mary said, "My soul

λελαλημένοις αὐτῇ παρὰ Κυρίου. Καὶ εἶπε Μαρι-
άμ· Μεγαλύνει ἡ ψυχή μου τὸν Κύριον, καὶ ἠγαλ-
λίασε τὸ πνεῦμά μου ἐπὶ Θεῷ τῷ σωτῆρί μου. Ὅ-
τι ἐπέβλεψεν ἐπὶ τὴν ταπείνωσιν τῆς δούλης αὐ-
τοῦ· ἰδοὺ γὰρ ἀπὸ τοῦ νῦν μακαριοῦσί με πᾶσαι
αἱ γενεαί. Ὅτι ἐποίησέ μοι μεγαλεῖα ὁ δυνατός,
καὶ ἅγιον τὸ ὄνομα αὐτοῦ. Ἔμεινε δὲ Μαριὰμ σὺν
αὐτῇ ὡσεὶ μῆνας τρεῖς, καὶ ὑπέστρεψεν εἰς τὸν οἶκον αὐτῆς.

Λαός: Δόξα σοι, Κύριε, δόξα σοι.

Ἦχος β΄

Δόξα Πατρὶ καὶ Υἱῷ καὶ Ἁγίῳ Πνεύματι.

Πάτερ Λόγε, Πνεῦμα, Τριὰς ἡ ἐν μονάδι, ἐξάλειψον τὰ πλήθη τῶν ἐμῶν ἐγκλημάτων.

*Pater Loge, Pnevma, Trias i en monadi, exsalip-
son ta plithi ton emon englimaton.*

Καὶ νῦν καὶ ἀεὶ καὶ εἰς τοὺς αἰῶνας τῶν αἰώνων.
Ἀμήν.

Ταῖς τῆς Θεοτόκου πρεσβείαις, Ἐλεῆμον, ἐ-
ξάλειψον τὰ πλήθη τῶν ἐμῶν ἐγκλημάτων.

*Tes tis Theotokou, presvies, Eleimon, exsalip-
son ta plithi ton emon englimaton.*

Ἱερεύς: Ἐλέησόν με ὁ Θεός, κατὰ τὸ μέγα ἔλεός
σου, καὶ κατὰ τὸ πλῆθος τῶν οἰκτιρμῶν σου ἐ-
ξάλειψον τὸ ἀνόμημά μου.

magnifies the Lord, and my spirit rejoices in God my Savior, for he has regarded the lowly estate of his handmaiden. For behold henceforth all generations will call me blessed; for he who is mighty has done great things for me, and holy is his name." And Mary remained with her about three months, and returned to her home.

People: Glory to You, O Lord, glory to You.

Tone 2.

Glory to the Fatherand the Son and the Holy Spirit.

Father, Word, and Spirit, Trinity in oneness, wash away my many personal offenses.

Now and for ever and to the ages of ages. Amen.

Through the intercessions of the Theotokos, merciful One, wash away my many personal offenses.

Verse: Have mercy upon me, O God, according to Your great mercy; and according to the multitude of Your compassions blot out my transgressions.

'Ηχος πλ. β΄ "Ολην ἀποθέμενοι.

Μὴ καταπιστεύσῃς με, ἀνθρωπίνῃ προστασίᾳ,
Παναγία Δέσποινα, ἀλλὰ δέξαι δέησιν τοῦ ἱκέτου
σου· θλῖψις γὰρ ἔχει με, φέρειν οὐ δύναμαι, τῶν
δαιμόνων τὰ τοξεύματα· σκέπην οὐ κέκτημαι, οὐ-
δὲ ποῦ προσφύγω ὁ ἄθλιος, πάντοθεν πολεμούμε-
νος καὶ παραμυθίαν οὐκ ἔχω πλήν σου, Δέσποινα τοῦ κόσμου, ἐλπὶς καὶ προστασία τῶν πιστῶν,
μή μου παρίδῃς τὴν δέησιν, τὸ συμφέρον ποίησον.

*Mi katapistefsis me, anthropini prostasia,
Panagia Despina, ala deje deisin tou iketou sou;
thlipsis gar ehi me, ferin ou dinami, ton demonon
ta toxsevmata; skepin ou kektime, oude pou pro-
sfigo o athlios, pandothen polemoumenos ke para-
mithian ouk eho plin sou, Despina tou kosmou, elpis
ke prostasia ton piston, mi mou paridis tin deisin,
to simferon piison.*

Θεοτοκία.

Οὐδεὶς προστρέχων ἐπὶ σοί, κατῃσχυμένος ἀ-
πὸ σοῦ ἐκπορεύεται, ἁγνὴ παρθένε Θεοτόκε· ἀλλ᾽
αἰτεῖται τὴν χάριν καὶ λαμβάνει τὸ δώρημα, πρὸς
τὸ συμφέρον τῆς αἰτήσεως.

*Oudis prostrehon epi si, katishimenos apo sou
ekporevete, agni parthene Theotoke; al etite tin harin
ke lamvani to dorima, pros to simferon tis etiseos.*

Plagal of the 2nd Tone

Put me not into the hands
Of any human protection,
O our Lady, most holy,
But do now receive the prayers of your supplicant;
Sorrow has taken me,
And I am unable
To withstand and bear the demon's darts;
Shelter I do not have,
Nor a place to go, worthless that I am;
Lady of humanity,
The shelter of the faithful and their hope,
Do not reject my prayers to you,
Do the things that profit me.

The Theotokia

No one is turned away from you,
Ashamed and empty, who flee unto you,
O pure virgin Theotokos;
But one asks for the favor,
And the gift is received from you,
To the advantage of their own request.

Μεταβολὴ τῶν θλιβομένων, ἀπαλλαγὴ τῶν ἀσθενούντων, ὑπάρχουσα Θεοτόκε παρθένε, σῶζε πόλιν καὶ λαόν, τῶν πολεμουμένων ἡ εἰρήνη, τῶν χειμαζομένων ἡ γαλήνη, ἡ μόνη προστασία τῶν πιστῶν.

Metavoli ton thlivomenon, apalagi ton asthenoundon, iparhousa, Theotoke parthene, soze polin ke laon, ton polemoumenon i irini, ton himazomenon i galini, i moni prostasia ton piston.

Ἱερεύς: Σῶσον ὁ Θεὸς τὸν λαόν σου, καὶ εὐλόγησον τὴν κληρονομίαν σου· ἐπίσκεψαι τὸν κόσμον σου ἐν ἐλέει καὶ οἰκτιρμοῖς· ὕψωσον κέρας Χριστιανῶν Ὀρθοδόξων, καὶ κατάπεμψον ἐφ᾽ ἡμᾶς τὰ ἐλέη σου τὰ πλούσια, πρεσβείαις τῆς Παναχράντου Δεσποίνης ἡμῶν Θεοτόκου καὶ ἀειπαρθένου Μαρίας, δυνάμει τοῦ τιμίου καὶ ζωοποιοῦ Σταυροῦ· προστασίαις τῶν τιμίων, ἐπουρανίων Δυνάμεων Ἀσωμάτων· ἱκεσίαις τοῦ τιμίου, ἐνδόξου, προφήτου, προδρόμου καὶ βαπτιστοῦ Ἰωάννου· τῶν ἁγίων ἐνδόξων καὶ πανευφήμων Ἀποστόλων· τῶν ἐν ἁγίοις πατέρων ἡμῶν μεγάλων Ἱεραρχῶν καὶ οἰκουμενικῶν Διδασκάλων, Βασιλείου τοῦ Μεγάλου, Γρηγορίου τοῦ Θεολόγου καὶ Ἰωάννου τοῦ Χρυσοστόμου, Ἀθανασίου καὶ Κυρίλλου, Ἰωάννου τοῦ Ἐλεήμονος, πατριαρχῶν Ἀλεξανδρείας, Νικολάου τοῦ ἐν Μύροις, Σπυρίδωνος ἐπισκόπου Τριμυθοῦντος, τῶν θαυματουργῶν· τῶν ἁγίων ἐνδόξων μεγαλομαρτύρων Γεωργίου τοῦ τροπαιοφόρου, Δημητρίου τοῦ μυροβλήτου, Θεοδώρου τοῦ Τήρωνος καὶ Θεοδώρου τοῦ

The transformation of the afflicted,
You are the cure of those in sickness,
Theotokos, O Virgin;
Save your people and your town.
You are the peace of those in conflict,
The calm of those in turmoil,
The only protection of the faithful.

Priest: O God, save Your People, and bless Your inheritance; look upon Your world with mercy and compassion; raise the Orthodox Christians to glory, and shower us with your abundant mercies, through the intercessions of our all-pure Lady, the Theotokos and ever-virgin Mary, through the power of the precious and life-giving Cross; through the protection of the honorable, heavenly bodiless powers; of the honorable, glorious prophet, the Forerunner John the Baptist; of the holy glorious and all-praised Apostles; of our holy fathers the great hierarchs and ecumenical teachers, Basil the Great, Gregory the Theologian, and John Chrysostom; Athanasios and Cyril, John the Merciful, patriarchs of Alexandria; Nicholas of Myra, Spyridon bishop of Trimythous, the wonder-workers; of the holy glorious great martyrs George the triumphant, Demetrios the myrrh-flowing, Theodore of Tyros and Theodore the Commander; of the holy-martyrs Charalambos and

Στρατηλάτου· τῶν ἱερομαρτύρων Χαραλάμπους καὶ Ἐλευθερίου· τῶν ἁγίων ἐνδόξων καὶ καλλινίκων Μαρτύρων· τῶν Ὁσίων καὶ θεοφόρων Πατέρων ἡμῶν· (τοῦ ἁγίου τοῦ ναοῦ, ἐφ᾽ ὅσον δὲν ἐμνημονεύθη ἐν τοῖς ἄνω)· τῶν ἁγίων καὶ δικαίων θεοπατόρων Ἰωακεὶμ καὶ Ἄννης, τοῦ Ἁγίου (Ὄνομα) καὶ πάντων σου τῶν ἁγίων· ἱκετεύομέν σε μόνε πολυέλεε Κύριε, ἐπάκουσον ἡμῶν τῶν ἁμαρτωλῶν δεομένων σου καὶ ἐλέησον ἡμᾶς.

Λαός: Κύριε, ἐλέησον (*12*).

Ἱερεύς: Ἐλέει καὶ οἰκτιρμοῖς, καὶ φιλανθρωπίᾳ τοῦ μονογενοῦς σου Υἱοῦ, μεθ᾽ οὗ εὐλογητὸς εἶ σὺν τῷ παναγίῳ καὶ ἀγαθῷ καὶ ζωοποιῷ σου Πνεύματι, νῦν καὶ ἀεὶ καὶ εἰς τοὺς αἰῶνας τῶν αἰώνων.

Λαός: Ἀμήν.

Ὠδὴ ζ᾽ Ὁ Εἱρμός.

Οἱ ἐκ τῆς Ἰουδαίας, καταντήσαντες παῖδες ἐν τῇ Βαβυλῶνι ποτέ, τῇ πίστει τῆς Τριάδος, τὴν φλόγα τῆς καμίνου, κατεπάτησαν ψάλλοντες· Ὁ τῶν πατέρων ἡμῶν, Θεὸς εὐλογητὸς εἶ.

I ek tis Ioudeas, katandisandes pedes en Vaviloni pote, ti pisti tis Triados, tin floga tis kaminou, katepatisan psalondes; o ton pateron imon, Theos evlogitos i.

Eleutherios; of the holy glorious triumphant Martyrs; of our pious and God-bearing Fathers; of (*the Saint of the Church*); of the holy and righteous Ancestors of God, Joachim and Anna; of Saint (*Name*) whose memory we celebrate today; and of all Your Saints, we beseech You Lord, Who alone are all merciful; hear the prayers of us sinners and have mercy upon us.

People: Lord, have mercy (*12*).

Priest: By the mercy and compassion, and love of Your only begotten Son, with whom You are blessed, together with Your all-holy and life giving Spirit, now and forever and to the ages of ages.

People: Amen.

Ode 7. The Heirmos

Coming out of Judea,
Once the young men did go to the land of Babylon;
The flame of the furnace,
They trampled down while chanting,
With their faith in the Trinity:
O the God of our Fathers,
Blessed are You, our God.

Ὑπεραγία Θεοτόκε σῶσον ἡμᾶς.

Τὴν ἡμῶν σωτηρίαν, ὡς ἠθέλησας, Σῶτερ οἰκονομήσασθαι, ἐν μήτρᾳ τῆς Παρθένου, κατῴκησας τῷ κόσμῳ, ἣν προστάτιν ἀνέδειξας· Ὁ τῶν πατέρων ἡμῶν Θεός, εὐλογητὸς εἶ.

Tin imon sotirian, os ithelisas, Soter ikonomisasthe, en mitra tis parhtenou, katokisas to kosmo, in prostatin anedixsas; O ton pateron imon Theos, evlogitos i.

Ὑπεραγία Θεοτόκε σῶσον ἡμᾶς.

Θελητὴν τοῦ ἐλέους, ὃν ἐγέννησας Μῆτερ ἁγνὴ δυσώπησον, ῥυσθῆναι, τῶν πταισμάτων, ψυχῆς τε μολυσμάτων, τοὺς ἐν πίστει κραυγάζοντας· Ὁ τῶν πατέρων ἡμῶν Θεός, εὐλογητὸς εἶ.

Thelitin tou eleous, on egenisas miter agni disopison, risthine ton ptesmaton, psihis te molismaton, tous en pisti kravgazondas;O ton pateron imon Theos, evlogitos i.

Δόξα Πατρὶ καὶ Υἱῷ καὶ Ἁγίῳ Πνεύματι.

Θησαυρὸν σωτηρίας καὶ πηγὴν ἀφθαρσίας τὴν σὲ κυήσασαν, καὶ πύργον ἀσφαλείας, καὶ θύραν μετανοίας, τοῖς κραυγάζουσιν ἔδειξας· Ὁ τῶν πατέρων ἡμῶν Θεός, εὐλογητὸς εἶ.

Thisavron sotirias ke pigin aftharsias tin se kiisasan, ke pirgon asfalias, ke thiran metanias, tis kravgazousin edixsas. O ton pateron imon Theos, evlogitos i.

Most Holy Theotokos, save us.

As You willed, O our Savior,
To dispense our salvation through Your economy
Inside the Virgin's womb;
You showed to all the people
That she was our own guardian;
O the God of our fathers,
Blessed are You, our God.

Most Holy Theotokos, save us.

The bestower of mercy
That you bore, O pure Mother, entreat on our
behalf;
From sins deliver us,
And from the soul's defilement,
We who cry out most faithfully:
O the God of our fathers,
Blessed are You, our God.

Glory to the Father and the Son and the Holy Spirit.

A fountain of pureness
And a tower of safety is she who carried You,
A treasure of salvation
And the door of repentance,
She has been shown to those that cry;
O the God of our fathers,
Blessed are You, our God.

Καὶ νῦν καὶ ἀεὶ καὶ εἰς τοὺς αἰῶνας τῶν αἰώνων. Ἀμήν.

Σωμάτων μαλακίας, καὶ ψυχῶν ἀρρωστίας Θεογεννήτρια, τῶν πόθῳ προσιόντων, τῇ σκέπῃ σου τῇ θείᾳ θεραπεύειν ἀξίωσον, ἡ τὸν Σωτῆρα Χριστὸν ἡμῖν ἀποτεκοῦσα.

Somaton malakias, ke psihon arosties Theoge-nitria, to potho prosiondon, ti skepi sou ti thia therapevin axsioson, i ton sotira Hriston imin apotekousa.

Ὠδὴ η΄ Ὁ Εἱρμός.

Τὸν Βασιλέα τῶν Οὐρανῶν, ὃν ὑμνοῦσι, στρατιαὶ τῶν Ἀγγέλων, ὑμνεῖτε καὶ ὑπερυψοῦτε, εἰς πάντας τοὺς αἰῶνας.

Ton Vasilea ton Ouranon, on imnousi, stratie ton angelon, imnite ke iperipsoute, is pandas tous eonas.

Ὑπεραγία Θεοτόκε σῶσον ἡμᾶς.

Τοὺς βοηθείας τῆς παρὰ σοῦ δεομένους, μὴ παρίδῃς Παρθένε, ὑμνοῦντας, καὶ ὑπερυψοῦντάς σε, Κόρη, εἰς αἰῶνας.

Tous voithias tis para sou deomenous, mi paridis Parthene, imnoundas ke iperipsoundas se Kori, is eonas.

Now and for ever and to the ages of ages. Amen.

The illnesses of body,
and the soul's ailing sickness, of those who run to
you.
For divine protection,
As God's holy Mother,
Make them worthy of remedy:
For the Savior Christ
Was born from you.

Ode 8. The Heirmos

The King of heaven, Who is praised,
And is hymned by the host of the angels;
Praise Him and exalt Him
Throughout the many ages.

Most holy Theotokos, save us.

Do not neglect those who seek the help you grant.
They hymn you, O Virgin Maiden,
And they do exalt you
Throughout the many ages.

Ὑπεραγία Θεοτόκε σῶσον ἡμᾶς.

Τῶν ἰαμάτων τὸ δαψιλὲς ἐπιχέεις τοῖς πιστῶς ὑμνοῦσι σε Παρθένε, καὶ ὑπερυψοῦσι, τὸν ἄφραστόν σου τόκον.

Ton iamaton to dapsiles epiheis tis pistos imnousi se Parthene, ke iperipsousi, ton afraston sou tokon.

Δόξα Πατρὶ καὶ Υἱῷ καὶ Ἁγίῳ Πνεύματι.

Τὰς ἀσθενείας μου τῆς ψυχῆς ἰατρεύεις, καὶ σαρκὸς τὰς ὀδύνας Παρθένε, ἵνα σὲ δοξάζω τὴν Κεχαριτωμένην.

Tas asthenias mou tis psihis iatrevis, ke sarkos tas odinas Parthene, ina se doxsazo tin keharitomenin.

Καὶ νῦν καὶ ἀεὶ καὶ εἰς τοὺς αἰῶνας τῶν αἰώνων. Ἀμήν.

Τῶν πειρασμῶν σὺ τὰς προσβολὰς ἐκδιώκεις, καὶ παθῶν τὰς ἐφόδους Παρθένε, ὅθεν σὲ ὑμνοῦμεν εἰς πάντας τοὺς αἰῶνας.

Ton pirasmon si tas prosvolas ekdiokis, ke pathon tas efodous Parthene, othen se imnoumen is pandas tous eonas.

Most Holy Theotokos, save us.

O Virgin, you pour a wealth of healing
On those who faithfully hymn you,
And those who exalt your
Childbearing wonder.

Glory to the Father and the Son and the Holy Spirit.

The infirmities of my soul are healed by you,
And the pains of my body, O Virgin,
So that I may praise you,
O Lady, in God's favor.

Now and for ever and to the ages of ages. Amen.

You drive away the assaults of temptations,
And attacks of the passions, O Virgin,
Therefore do we praise you
Throughout the many ages.

'Ωδὴ θ' Ὁ Εἱρμός.

Κυρίως Θεοτόκον, σὲ ὁμολογοῦμεν οἱ διὰ σοῦ σε-
σωσμένοι, Παρθένε ἁγνή, σὺν Ἀσωμάτοις χορεί-
αις, σὲ μεγαλύνοντες.

*Kirios Theotokon, se omologoumen i dia sou se-
sosmeni, Parthene agni, sin Asomatis hories, se
megalinondes.*

Ὑπεραγία Θεοτόκε, σῶσον ἡμᾶς.

Ροήν μου τῶν δακρύων μὴ ἀποποιήσῃς, ἡ τὸν
παντὸς ἐκ προσώπου, πᾶν δάκρυον, ἀφῃρηκότα
Παρθένε, Χριστὸν κυήσασα.

*Roin mou ton dakrion, mi apopiisis, i ton pan-
dos ek prosopou, pan dakrion afirikota Parthene,
Hriston kiisasa.*

Ὑπεραγία Θεοτόκε, σῶσον ἡμᾶς.

Χαρᾶς μου τὴν καρδίαν, πλήρωσον Παρθένε,
ἡ τῆς χαρᾶς δεξαμένη τὸ πλήρωμα, τῆς ἁμαρτίας
τὴν λύπην ἐξαφανίσασα.

*Haras mou tin kardian, pliroson Parthene, i tis
haras dexsameni to pliroma, tis amartias tin lipin
exsafanisasa.*

Ode 9. The Heirmos.

Saved through you, O pure Virgin,
Hence we do confess you
To be most truly the birthgiver of our Lord;
With choirs of bodiless Angels,
You do we magnify.

Most Holy Theotokos, save us.

The streams of my many tears,
Reject not, Holy Virgin;
For you gave birth to the One who dried all the tears,
From all the faces of people;
The Christ was born of you.

Most holy Theotokos, save us.

With gladness fill my heart,
Most holy Virgin lady,
For you are she who received the abundant joy;
Take the grief of my sinfulness,
And make it disappear.

Ὑπεραγία Θεοτόκε, σῶσον ἡμᾶς.

Λιμὴν καὶ προστασία, τῶν σοὶ προσφευγόντων, γενοῦ Παρθένε, καὶ τεῖχος ἀκράδαντον, καταφυγή τε καὶ σκέπη καὶ ἀγαλλίαμα.

Limin ke prostasia, ton si prosfevgondon, genou Parthene, ke tihos akradandon, katafigi te ke skepi ke agaliama.

Δόξα Πατρὶ καὶ Υἱῷ καὶ Ἁγίῳ Πνεύματι.

Φωτός σου ταῖς ἀκτῖσι, λάμπρυνον Παρθένε, τὸ ζοφερὸν τῆς ἀγνοίας διώκουσα, τοὺς εὐσεβῶς Θεοτόκον σὲ καταγγέλλοντας.

Fotos sou tes aktisi, lamprinon Parthene, to zoferon tis agnias diokousa, touw efsevos Theotokon se katangelondas.

Καὶ νῦν καὶ ἀεὶ καὶ εἰς τοὺς αἰῶνας τῶν αἰώνων. Ἀμήν.

Κακώσεως ἐν τόπῳ, τῷ τῆς ἀσθενείας ταπεινωθέντα, Παρθένε θεράπευσον, ἐξ ἀρρωστίας εἰς ῥῶσιν μετασκευάζουσα.

Kakoseos en topo to tis asthenias tapinothenda, Parthene therapefson, ex arostias is rosin metaskevazousa.

Most Holy Theotokos, save us.

A shelter and protection
And a wall unshaken,
Become, O Virgin, for those who flee to you,
A sheltered cover and refuge,
And a place of joy.

Glory to the Father and the Son and the Holy Spirit.

O Virgin, from the brightness
Of your light illumine
The ones who call you most piously Mother of God,
Take all the gloom of our ignorance
And banish it away.

Now and forever and to the ages of ages. Amen.

Oppressed I am, O Virgin;
In a place of sickness,
I have been humbled; I ask you: bring remedy,
Transform my illness, my sickness,
Into a wholesomeness.

Ἄξιόν ἐστιν ὡς ἀληθῶς, μακαρίζειν σε τὴν Θεοτόκον, τὴν ἀειμακάριστον καὶ παναμώμητον καὶ μητέρα τοῦ Θεοῦ ἡμῶν.

Axsion estin os alithos, makarizin se tin Theotokon, tin aimakariston ke panamomiton ke mitera tou Theou imon.

Τὴν τιμιωτέραν τῶν Χερουβεὶμ καὶ ἐνδοξοτέραν ἀσυγκρίτως τῶν Σεραφείμ, τὴν ἀδιαφθόρως Θεὸν Λόγον τεκοῦσαν· τὴν ὄντως Θεοτόκον σὲ μεγαλύνομεν.

Tin timioteran ton Herouvim ke endoxsoteran asingritos ton Serafim tin adiafthoros Theon Logon tekousan; tin ondos Theotokon se megalinomen.

(Καὶ θυμιᾷ ὁ Ἱερεὺς τὸ Θυσιαστήριον καὶ τὸν Λαόν, ἢ τὸν οἶκον ὅπου ψάλλεται ἡ Παράκλησις· καὶ ἡμεῖς ψάλλομεν τὰ παρόντα Μεγαλυνάρια.)

Τὴν ὑψηλοτέραν τῶν οὐρανῶν, καὶ καθαρωτέραν λαμπηδόνων ἡλιακῶν, τὴν λυτρωσαμένην ἡμᾶς ἐκ τῆς κατάρας, τὴν Δέσποιναν τοῦ κόσμου, ὕμνοις τιμήσωμεν.

Tin ipsiloteran ton ouranon, ke katharoteran lampidonon iliakon, tin litrosamenin imas ek tis kataras, tin Despina tou kosmou, imnis timisomen.

Truly you are worthy to be blessed,
Mother of our God, the Theotokos,
You the ever blessed one, and all blameless one,
And the Mother of our God.

You are honored more than the Cherubim,
And you have more glory, when compared, to the
Seraphim;
You, without corruption,
Did bear God, the Logos;
You are the Theotokos;
You do we magnify.

*(The priest censes the altar and the people, or the place
where the Paraklesis is held, while we chant the following megalynaria.)*

Higher than the heavens above are you,
And you are much purer
Than the radiance of the sun;
You who have redeemed us
From the curse which is upon us;
The Lady of all people,
In hymns, do we honor you.

Ἀπὸ τῶν πολλῶν μου ἁμαρτιῶν, ἀσθενεῖ τὸ σῶμα, ἀσθενεῖ μου καὶ ἡ ψυχή· πρὸς σὲ καταφεύγω τὴν Κεχαριτωμένην· ἐλπὶς ἀπηλπισμένων, σύ μοι βοήθησον.

Apo ton polon mou amartion, astheni to soma, astheni mou ke i psihi; pros se katafevgo tin Keharitomenin; elpis apilpizmenon, si mi voithison.

Δέσποινα καὶ μήτηρ τοῦ Λυτρωτοῦ, δέξαι παρακλήσεις ἀναξίων σῶν ἱκετῶν, ἵνα μεσιτεύσῃς πρὸς τὸν ἐκ σοῦ τεχθέντα· Ὦ Δέσποινα τοῦ κόσμου, γενοῦ μεσίτρια.

Despina ke mitir tou Litrotou, dexse paraklisis anaxsion son iketon, ina mesitefsis pros ton ek sou tehthenda; O Despina tou kosmou, genou mesitria.

Ψάλλομεν προθύμως σοι τὴν ᾠδήν, νῦν τῇ πανυμνήτῳ, Θεοτόκῳ χαρμονικῶς· μετὰ τοῦ Προδρόμου, καὶ πάντων τῶν Ἁγίων, δυσώπει Θεοτόκε, τοῦ οἰκτειρῆσαι ἡμᾶς.

Psalomen prothimos si tin odin, nin ti panimnito Theotoko, harmonikos meta tou Prodromou, ke pandon ton Agion, disopi Theotoke, tou iktirise imas.

From the great multitude of my sins,
Ill am I in body,
Ill am I also in my soul;
I am fleeing to you,
The one who is all-blessed,
The hope of all the hopeless,
Please come bring help to me.

Lady and the Mother of Him who saves,
Receive the supplications
Of the lowly who pray to you;
Mediate between us
And the One you brought forth;
O Lady of all people,
Intercede for us.

Now with zeal we chant this Ode to you;
You, the all-praised Lady,
Theotokos, we hymn with joy;
With the saints most holy,
Together with the Baptist,
Beseech, O Theotokos,
For God's mercy on us.

Ἄλαλα τὰ χείλη τῶν ἀσεβῶν, τῶν μὴ προσκυνούντων, τὴν εἰκόνα σου τὴν σεπτήν, τὴν ἱστορηθεῖσαν ὑπὸ τοῦ ἀποστόλου, Λουκᾶ ἱερωτάτου, τὴν Ὁδηγήτριαν.

Alala ta hili ton asevon ton mi proskinoundon, tin ikona sou tin septin, tin istorithisan ipo tou apostolou, Louka ierotatou, tin Odigitrian.

(*Τὸ Μεγαλυνάριον τοῦ Ἁγίου τοῦ Ναοῦ. Εἶτα:*)

Πᾶσαι τῶν ἀγγέλων αἱ στρατιαί, Πρόδρομε Κυρίου, Ἀποστόλων ἡ δωδεκάς, οἱ Ἅγιοι Πάντες μετὰ τῆς Θεοτόκου, ποιήσατε πρεσβείαν, εἰς τὸ σωθῆναι ἡμᾶς.

Pase ton angelon e stratie, Prodrome Kiriou, Apostolon i dodekas. i agii Pandes meta tis Theotokou, piisate presvian is to sothine imas.

Speechless be the lips of impious ones,
Those who do not reverence
Your great icon, the sacred one
Which is called Directress,
And was depicted for us
By one of the apostles,
Luke the Evangelist.

(The Megalynarion of the church is chanted. Then:)

With the hosts of Angels, God's messengers,
With the Lord's Forerunner,
And Apostles, the chosen twelve,
With the saints most holy,
And with you, the Theotokos,
We seek your intercession
For our salvation.

Λαός: Ἅγιος ὁ Θεός, Ἅγιος Ἰσχυρός, Ἅγιος Ἀθάνατος ἐλέησον ἡμᾶς. *(3)*

Δόξα Πατρὶ καὶ Υἱῷ καὶ Ἁγίῳ Πνεύματι. Καὶ νῦν καὶ ἀεὶ καὶ εἰς τοὺς αἰῶνας τῶν αἰώνων. Ἀμήν.

Παναγία Τριάς, ἐλέησον ἡμᾶς· Κύριε, ἱλάσθητι ταῖς ἁμαρτίαις ἡμῶν. Δέσποτα, συγχώρησον τὰς ἀνομίας ἡμῖν. Ἅγιε, ἐπίσκεψαι καὶ ἴασαι τὰς ἀσθενείας ἡμῶν, ἕνεκεν τοῦ ὀνόματός σου.

Κύριε, ἐλέησον· Κύριε, ἐλέησον· Κύριε, ἐλέησον.

Δόξα Πατρὶ καὶ Υἱῷ καὶ Ἁγίῳ Πνεύματι. Καὶ νῦν καὶ ἀεὶ καὶ εἰς τοὺς αἰῶνας τῶν αἰώνων. Ἀμήν.

Πάτερ ἡμῶν ὁ ἐν τοῖς οὐρανοῖς, ἁγιασθήτω τὸ ὄνομά σου. Ἐλθέτω ἡ βασιλεία σου. Γενηθήτω τὸ θέλημά σου, ὡς ἐν οὐρανῷ, καὶ ἐπὶ τῆς γῆς. Τὸν ἄρτον ἡμῶν τὸν ἐπιούσιον δὸς ἡμῖν σήμερον. Καὶ ἄφες ἡμῖν τὰ ὀφειλήματα ἡμῶν, ὡς καὶ ἡμεῖς ἀφίεμεν τοῖς ὀφειλέταις ἡμῶν. Καὶ μὴ εἰσενέγκῃς ἡμᾶς εἰς πειρασμόν, ἀλλὰ ῥῦσαι ἡμᾶς ἀπὸ τοῦ πονηροῦ.

Ἱερεύς: Ὅτι σοῦ ἐστιν ἡ βασιλεία καὶ ἡ δύναμις καὶ ἡ δόξα, τοῦ Πατρὸς καὶ τοῦ Υἱοῦ καὶ τοῦ Ἁγίου Πνεύματος, νῦν καὶ ἀεὶ καὶ εἰς τοὺς αἰῶνας τῶν αἰώνων. Ἀμήν.

People: Holy God, Holy Mighty, Holy Immortal, have mercy upon us (3).

Glory to the Father and the Son and the Holy Spirit, now and forever and to the ages of ages. Amen.

Most holy Trinity, have mercy upon us; Lord, pardon our sins; Master, forgive our transgressions; Holy One, visit and heal our infirrnities, for Your name's sake.

Lord have mercy (3).

Glory to the Father, and the Son and the Holy Spirit, now and forever and to the ages of ages. Amen.

Our Father, Who art in heaven, hallowed be Thy name. Thy kingdom come, Thy will be done, on earth as it is in heaven. Give us this day our daily bread; and forgive us our trespasses as we forgive those who trespass against us. And lead us not into temptation, but deliver us from evil.

Priest: For Yours is the kingdom and the power and the glory, of the Father and the Son and the Holy Spirit, now and forever and to the ages of ages. Amen.

(Μετὰ τὰ Τροπάρια ταῦτα.)
Ἦχος πλ. β΄

Ἐλέησον ἡμᾶς, Κύριε, ἐλέησον ἡμᾶς· πάσης γὰρ ἀπολογίας ἀποροῦντες, ταύτην σοι τὴν ἱκεσίαν ὡς Δεσπότῃ, οἱ ἁμαρτωλοὶ προσφέρομεν· ἐλέησον ἡμᾶς.

Eleison imas Kirie, eleison imas: pasis gar apologias aporoundes, taftin si tin ikesian os Despoti, i amartoli prosferomen; eleison imas.

Δόξα Πατρὶ καὶ Υἱῷ καὶ Ἁγίῳ Πνεύματι.

Κύριε, ἐλέησον ἡμᾶς· ἐπὶ σοὶ γὰρ πεποίθαμεν· Μὴ ὀργισθῇς ἡμῖν σφόδρα, μηδὲ μνησθῇς τῶν ἀνομιῶν ἡμῶν· ἀλλ᾽ ἐπίβλεψον καὶ νῦν ὡς εὔσπλαγχνος καὶ λύτρωσαι ἡμᾶς ἐκ τῶν ἐχθρῶν ἡμῶν· Σὺ γὰρ εἶ Θεὸς ἡμῶν, καὶ ἡμεῖς λαός σου· πάντες ἔργα χειρῶν σου, καὶ τὸ ὄνομά σου ἐπικεκλήμεθα.

Kirie eleison imas epi si gar pepithamen. Mi orgisthis imin sfodra, mide mnisthis ton anomion imon, al epivlepson ke nin os efsplahnos, ke litrose imas ek ton ehthron imon. si gar i Theos imon, ke imis laos sou; pandes gar erga hiron sou, ke to onoma sou epikeklimetha.

Have mercy on us, O Lord, have mercy on us,
For we are empty of all defense,
As sinners we offer this supplication to You;
O Master, have mercy on us.

Glory to the Father and the Son and the Holy Spirit.

Lord, have mercy on us,
For in You we have put our trust;
Be not exceedingly angry with us,
Nor remember our many iniquities;
But look upon us now as the Compassionate,
And deliver us from our enemies;
For You are our God, and we Your people,
We are all the work of Your hands,
And upon Your Name we have now called.

Καὶ νῦν καὶ ἀεὶ καὶ εἰς τοὺς αἰῶνας τῶν αἰώνων. Ἀμήν.

Θεοτοκίον

Τῆς εὐσπλαγχνίας τὴν πύλην ἄνοιξον ἡμῖν, εὐλογημένη Θεοτόκε· ἐλπίζοντες εἰς σέ, μὴ ἀστοχήσωμεν, ρυσθείημεν διὰ σοῦ τῶν περιστάσεων· σὺ γὰρ εἶ ἡ σωτηρία τοῦ γένους τῶν Χριστιανῶν.

Tis efsplahnias tin pilin anixon imin evlogimeni Theotoke; elpizondes is se, mi astohisomen; risthiimen dia sou ton peristaseon; si gar i i sotiria tou genous ton Hristianon.

(Κατὰ τὴν περίοδον τῶν Παρακλήσεων τοῦ Δεκαπενταυγούστου, ἀντὶ τῶν ἀνωτέρω τροπαρίων ψάλλονται: Τὸ Ἀπολυτίκιον τοῦ Ἁγίου τῆς ἡμέρας καὶ τὸ Θεοτοκίον τοῦ αὐτοῦ ἤχου.)

Ἱερεύς: Ἐλέησον ἡμᾶς ὁ Θεός, κατὰ τὸ μέγα ἔλεος σου, δεόμεθά σου, ἐπάκουσον καὶ ἐλέησον.

Λαός: Κύριε, ἐλέησον (3).

Ἱερεύς: Ἔτι δεόμεθα ὑπὲρ τοῦ Ἀρχιεπισκόπου ἡμῶν (ὄνομα) καὶ τοῦ Ἐπισκόπου ἡμῶν (ὄνομα) καὶ πάσης τῆς ἐν Χριστῷ ἡμῶν ἀδελφότητος.

Λαός: Κύριε, ἐλέησον (3).

Now and for ever and to the ages of ages. Amen.

The Theotokion

The doors of caring do now open unto us,
O most blessed Theotokos,
So that hoping in you we shall not fail;
Through you we may be delivered from adversities,
For you are the salvation of the Christian faith.

*(During the period from the 1st to the 14th of August,
instead of the above Troparia, the Apolytikion of the day
and the Theotokion of the tone are chanted.)*

Priest: Have mercy on us, O God, according to your
great love, we pray to you, hear us, and have mercy.

People: Lord, have mercy (*3*).

Priest: Again we pray for our Archbishop (*name*),
and our Bishop (*name*), and all the clergy and the
laity in Christ.

People: Lord, have mercy (*3*).

Ἱερεύς: Ἔτι δεόμεθα ὑπὲρ ἐλέους, ζωῆς, εἰρήνης, ὑγείας σωτηρίας, ἐπισκέψεως, συγχωρήσεως καὶ ἀφέσεως τῶν ἁμαρτιῶν τῶν δούλων τοῦ Θεοῦ, πάντων τῶν εὐσεβῶν καὶ ὀρθοδόξων χριστιανῶν, τῶν κατοικούντων καὶ παρεπιδημούντων ἐν τῇ πόλει *(ἢ νήσῳ)* ταύτῃ, τῶν ἐνοριτῶν, ἐπιτρόπων, συνδρομητῶν καὶ ἀφιερωτῶν τοῦ ἁγίου Ναοῦ τούτου.
Λαός: Κύριε, ἐλέησον (3).

Ἱερεύς: Ἔτι δεόμεθα καὶ ὑπὲρ τῶν δούλων τοῦ Θεοῦ *(καὶ μνημονεύει ὀνομαστὶ τῶν δι᾽ οὓς ἡ Παράκλησις τελεῖται.)*
Λαός: Κύριε, ἐλέησον (3).

Ἱερεύς: Ἔτι δεόμεθα ὑπὲρ τοῦ διαφυλαχθῆναι τὴν ἁγίαν Ἐκκλησίαν καὶ τὴν πόλιν *(ἢ χώραν, ἢ νῆσον)* ταύτην, καὶ πᾶσαν πόλιν καὶ χώραν ἀπὸ ὀργῆς, λοιμοῦ, λιμοῦ, σεισμοῦ, καταποντισμοῦ, πυρός, μαχαίρας, ἐπιδρομῆς ἀλλοφύλων, ἐμφυλίου πολέμου, καὶ αἰφνιδίου θανάτου· ὑπὲρ τὸν ἵλεων, εὐμενῆ καὶ εὐδιάλακτον, γενέσθαι τὸν ἀγαθὸν καὶ φιλάνθρωπον Θεὸν ἡμῶν, τοῦ ἀποστρέψαι καὶ διασκεδάσαι πᾶσαν ὀργὴν καὶ νόσον, τὴν καθ᾽ ἡμῶν κινουμένην· καὶ ῥύσασθαι ἡμᾶς ἐκ τῆς ἐπικειμένης δικαίας αὐτοῦ ἀπειλῆς, καὶ ἐλεῆσαι ἡμᾶς.
Λαός: Κύριε, ἐλέησον (3).

Ἱερεύς: Ἔτι δεόμεθα ὑπὲρ τοῦ εἰσακοῦσαι Κύριον τὸν Θεὸν φωνῆς τῆς δεήσεως ἡμῶν τῶν ἁμαρτωλῶν, καὶ ἐλεῆσαι ἡμᾶς.
Λαός: Κύριε, ἐλέησον (3).

Ἱερεύς: Ἐπάκουσον ἡμῶν, ὁ Θεός, ὁ Σωτὴρ ἡμῶν, ἡ ἐλπὶς πάντων τῶν περάτων τῆς γῆς καὶ τῶν ἐν θαλάσσῃ μακράν· καὶ ἵλεως, ἵλεως γενοῦ ἡμῖν, Δέσποτα ἐπὶ ταῖς ἁμαρτίαις ἡμῶν, καὶ ἐλέησον ἡμᾶς.

Priest: Again we pray for mercy, life, peace, health, salvation, visitation, forgiveness, and remission of the sins of the servants of God, all pious and Orthodox Christians, those who reside and visit in this city, the members, council members, contributors, and benefactors of this holy church.

People: Lord, have mercy (*3*).

Priest: Again we pray for the servants of God. . .(*at this time the Priest commemorates those for whom the Paraklesis is sung.*)

People: Lord, have mercy (*3*).

Priest: Again we pray for the safekeeping of this holy church and this city, and of all cities and towns from pestilence, famine, earthquake, flood, fire and the sword, from invasion of enemies, civil war, and unforeseen death; for His mercy, that He will be kind to entreat as our good God, Who loves all people and that He may turn away and scatter all wrath and disease that moves against us, and deliver us from His impending, justified chastisement, and have mercy on us.

People: Lord, have mercy (*3*).

Priest: Again we pray that the Lord God will hear the voices of the petitions of us sinners and have mercy on us.

People: Lord, have mercy (*3*).

Priest: Hear us, O God, our Savior, the hope of all the ends of the earth, and of those who are far off upon the sea; and show compassion on us, O Master, on our many sins, and have mercy upon us.

Λαός: Κύριε, ἐλέησον (3).

Ἐλεήμων γὰρ καὶ φιλάνθρωπος Θεὸς ὑπάρχεις, καὶ σοὶ τὴν δόξαν ἀναπέμπομεν, τῷ Πατρὶ καὶ τῷ Υἱῷ καὶ τῷ Ἁγίῳ Πνεύματι, νῦν καὶ ἀεὶ καὶ εἰς τοὺς αἰῶνας τῶν αἰώνων.
Λαός: Ἀμήν.

Ἱερεύς: Δόξα σοι Χριστὲ ὁ Θεός, ἡ ἐλπὶς ἡμῶν, δόξα σοι. Χριστὸς ὁ ἀληθινὸς Θεὸς ἡμῶν, ταῖς πρεσβείαις τῆς παναχράντου καὶ παναμώμου ἁγίας αὐτοῦ Μητρός· τῶν ἁγίων ἐνδόξων καὶ πανευφήμων Ἀποστόλων· τῶν ἁγίων ἐνδόξων καὶ καλλινίκων μαρτύρων· *(τοῦ ἁγίου τοῦ Ναοῦ)·* τῶν ἁγίων καὶ δικαίων θεοπατόρων Ἰωακεὶμ καὶ Ἄννης, τοῦ Ἁγίου *(Ὄνομα)*, οὗ τὴν μνήμην ἐπιτελοῦμεν, καὶ πάντων τῶν Ἁγίων, ἐλεῆσαι καὶ σῶσαι ἡμᾶς, ὡς ἀγαθὸς καὶ φιλάνθρωπος.

(Τῶν Χριστιανῶν ἀσπαζομένων τὴν εἰκόνα τῆς Θεοτόκου, ψάλλονται τὰ παρόντα Τροπάρια.)

Ἦχος β΄ Ὅτε ἐκ τοῦ ξύλου.

Πάντων προστατεύεις Ἀγαθή, τῶν καταφευγόντων ἐν πίστει, τῇ κραταιᾷ σου χειρί· ἄλλην γὰρ οὐκ ἔχομεν, ἁμαρτωλοὶ πρὸς Θεόν, ἐν κινδύνοις καὶ θλίψεσιν, ἀεὶ μεσιτείαν, οἱ κατακαμπτόμενοι, ὑπὸ πταισμάτων πολλῶν. Μῆτερ τοῦ Θεοῦ τοῦ Ὑψίστου· ὅθεν σοι προσπίπτομεν· Ῥῦσαι πάσης περιστάσεως τοὺς δούλους σου.

Pandon prostatevis agathi, ton katafevgondon en pisti, ti kratea sou hiri; alin gar ouk ehomen, a-martoli pros Theon, en kindinis ke thlipsesin, ai mesitian, i katakamptomeni ipo ptesmaton polon. Miter tou Theou tou Ipsistou; othen si prospiptomen; Rise, pasis peristaseos tous doulous sou.

People: Lord, have mercy (3).

Priest: For you are a merciful and loving God, and to You we give glory, to the Father and the Son and the Holy Spirit, now and forever and to the ages of the ages.

People: Amen.

Glory to You, O God, our hope, glory to You. May Christ our true God, through the intercessions of Your all-pure and blameless holy Mother; of the holy glorious and praise-worthy Apostles; of the holy glorious and triumphant martyrs; of (*the Saint of the Church*); of the holy righteous ancestors of God Joachim and Anna; of Saint (*name*) whose memory we celebrate today; and of all the Saints, have mercy and save us, as a good and loving God.

The Christian faithful reverence the icon of the Theotokos while the following troparia are chanted.

Tone 2.

All those
Do you shelter, O Good One,
Those who in their faith flee unto you,
With your strong hand, you protect;
We who sin have no one else,
Who intercedes for us
Before God, praying endlessly,
In ills and all dangers,
For us who are laiden with
Our many sins and mistakes;
Mother, of our God in the Highest
Therefore, we fall down to you, humbly;
From all the misfortunes, keep your servants safe.

Ὅμοιον.

Πάντων θλιβομένων ἡ χαρά, καὶ ἀδικουμένων προστάτις, καὶ πενομένων τροφή, ξένων τε παράκλησις, καὶ βακτηρία τυφλῶν, ἀσθενούντων ἐπίσκεψις, καταπονουμένων σκέπη καὶ ἀντίληψις, καὶ ὀρφανῶν βοηθός, Μῆτερ τοῦ Θεοῦ τοῦ Ὑψίστου, σὺ ὑπάρχεις· Ἄχραντε, σπεῦσον δυσωποῦμεν, ῥύσασθαι τοὺς δούλους σου.

Pandon thlivomenon i hara, ke adikoumenon prostatis, ke penomenon trofi, xsenon te paraklisis, ke vaktiria tiflon, asthenoundon episkepsis, kataponoumenon skepsis ke antilipsis, ke orfanon voithos, Miter tou Theou tou Ipsistou, si iparhis; Ahrande spefson disopoumen, risasthe tous doulous sou.

Ἦχος πλ. δ΄

Δέσποινα πρόσδεξαι τὰς δεήσεις τῶν δούλων σου, καὶ λύτρωσαι ἡμᾶς, ἀπὸ πάσης ἀνάγκης καὶ θλίψεως.

Despina prosdexse tas deisis ton doulon sou ke litrose imas apo pasis anangis ke thlipseos.

Ἦχος β΄

Τὴν πᾶσαν ἐλπίδα μου εἰς σὲ ἀνατίθημι, Μήτηρ τοῦ Θεοῦ· φύλαξόν με ὑπὸ τὴν σκέπην σου.

Tin pasan elpida mou is se anatithimi, Mitir tou Theou; filaxson me ipo tin skepin sou.

The same

For those
In great sorrow you are joy,
And for the oppressed, a protection,
And for the hungry, their food,
Comfort unto those estranged;
You are a staff to the blind,
Visitation of all those sick,
And to those held by pain
Shelter and a comforting,
And to the orphaned, an aid;
Mother, of our God in the highest,
You who are the Spotless One, hasten,
Save your servants from their sin, we ask of you.

Plagal of the 4th Tone

Lady, do you receive,
From your servants, their many prayers;
And deliver all of us,
From all sadness and necessity.

Tone 2

My numerous hopes are placed
Before you, most holy One;
Mother of our God,
Guard me with care, within your sheltered arms.

Κατὰ τὴν περίοδον τοῦ Δεκαπενταυγούστου εἴθισται νὰ ψάλλωνται, ἀντὶ τῶν ἀνωτέρω Θεοτοκίων, τὰ ἑξῆς Ἐξαποστειλάρια.

Ἦχος γ΄

Ἀπόστολοι ἐκ περάτων, συναθροισθέντες ἐνθάδε, Γεθσημανῇ τῷ χωρίῳ, κηδεύσατέ μου τὸ σῶμα· καὶ σύ, Υἱὲ καὶ Θεέ μου, παράλαβέ μου τὸ πνεῦμα.

Apostoli ek peraton, sinathristhendes enthade en Gethsimani to horio, kidefsate mou to soma; ke si Ie mou ke Thee mou, paralave mou to pnevma.

Ὁ γλυκασμὸς τῶν Ἀγγέλων, τῶν θλιβομένων ἡ χαρά, Χριστιανῶν ἡ προστάτις, Παρθένε μήτηρ Κυρίου, ἀντιλαβοῦ μου καὶ ῥῦσαι τῶν αἰωνίων βασάνων.

O glikasmos ton Angelon, ton thlivomenon i hara, Hristianon i prostatis; Parthene Mitir Kiriou, andilavou ke rise ton eonion basanon.

Καὶ σὲ μεσίτριαν ἔχω, πρὸς τὸν φιλάνθρωπον Θεόν· μή μου ἐλέγξῃ τὰς πράξεις, ἐνώπιον τῶν Ἀγγέλων· παρακαλῶ σε, Παρθένε, βοήθησόν μοι ἐν τάχει.

Ke se mesitrian, eho, pros ton filanthropon Theon; mi mou elegxsi tas praxsis, enopion ton Angelon; parakalo se Parthene, voithison mi en tahi.

*During the period from the 1st to the 15th of August,
instead of chanting the previous Theotokion, we chant
the following Exsapostilaria:*

Tone 3.
O You Apostles from far off,
Being gathered together
in the village of Gethsemane,
Lay my body in burial,
And You, my Son, and my God,
Receive now my spirit from me.

You are the sweetness of Angels,
The gladness of the afflicted ones,
A protection of all Christians,
O Virgin Mother of our Lord;
Grant me now help and save me
From the eternal torments.

I have you as Mediator
Before God who loves mankind;
May He not question my action
Before the hosts of the Angels,
I ask of you, O Virgin,
Hasten now quickly to my aid.

Χρυσοπλοκώτατε πύργε, καὶ δωδεκάτειχε πόλις, ἡλιοστάλακτε θρόνε, καθέδρα τοῦ βασιλέως, ἀκατανόητον θαῦμα, πῶς γαλουχεῖς τὸν Δεσπότην;

Hrisoplokotate pirge, ke dodekatihe polis, iliostalakte throne, kathedra tou vasileos akatanoiton thavma; pos galouhis ton Despotin?

Ἱερεύς: Δι' εὐχῶν τῶν ἁγίων πατέρων ἡμῶν, Κύριε Ἰησοῦ Χριστὲ ὁ Θεός, ἐλέησον καὶ σῶσον ἡμᾶς. Ἀμήν.

You are a tower adorned with gold,
A city surrounded by twelve walls,
A shining throne touched by the sun,
A royal seat for the King,
O unexplainable wonder,
How do you nurse the Master?

Priest: Through the prayers of our Holy Fathers,
Lord Jesus Christ, our God, have mercy and save us.

ISBN 0-917651-01-4

90000